# HOW NETWORKS WORK

## Critical Acclaim for other titles in the How It Works Series

"A real book, and quite a handsome one…The artwork, by Mr. Timothy Edward Downs, is striking and informative, and the text by Mr. White, executive editor of [*PC/Computing*], is very lucid."

—**L.R. Shannon,** *New York Times*

"As an enjoyable way to learn what makes your system tick, nothing comes close to *How Computers Work.* Browse through it for an entertaining and informative diversion, or work your way through from cover to cover for a thorough orientation. And when you're finished, don't hide it away on some remote shelf—leave it out on your coffee table where everyone can enjoy this beautiful book."

—**Alfred Poor,** *PC Magazine*

"Read *[PC/Computing] How Computers Work* to learn about the inner workings of the IBM and PC-compatible."

—**Ronald Rosenberg,** *Boston Globe*

"…a magnificently seamless integration of text and graphics that makes the complicated physics of the personal computer seem as obvious as gravity. When a book really pleases you—and this one does—there's a tendency to gush, so let's put it this way: I haven't seen any better explanations written (including my own) of how a PC works and why."

—**Larry Blasko,** *The Associated Press*

"If you're curious but fear computerese might get in the way, this book's the answer… it's an accessible, informative introduction that spreads everything out for logical inspection. To make everything even clearer, White introduces the explanatory diagrams with a few concise, lucid paragraphs of text. Readers will come away knowing not only what everything looks like but also what it does."

—**Stephanie Zvirin,** *Booklist*

"Computer users at all levels will enjoy and profit from this book."

—**Don Mills,** *Computing Now!*

# HOW NETWORKS WORK

FRANK J. DERFLER, JR.,
AND LES FREED

Illustrated by
MICHAEL TROLLER

**Ziff-Davis Press**
**Emeryville, California**

| Senior Development Editor | Melinda E. Levine |
| Technical Reviewer | Joe Salemi |
| Proofreader | Kayla Sussell |
| Cover Designer | Carrie English |
| Cover Illustrator | Michael Troller |
| Series Book Designer | Carrie English |
| Illustrator | Michael Troller |
| Layout Artist | Bruce Lundquist |
| Digital Prepress Specialist | Joe Schneider |
| Word Processors | Howard Blechman, Cat Haglund, and Allison Levin |
| Indexer | David C. Heiret |

Ziff-Davis Press books are produced on a Macintosh computer system with the following applications: FrameMaker®, Microsoft® Word, QuarkXPress®, Adobe Illustrator®, Adobe Photoshop®, Adobe Streamline™, MacLink®Plus, Aldus® FreeHand™, Collage Plus™.

Ziff-Davis Press
5903 Christie Avenue
Emeryville, CA 94608

ISBN 1-56276-129-3

Manufactured in the United States of America
10 9 8 7 6 5 4 3 2

# PART 1

## Communication by Wire
1

# PART 2

## Computers and Telephones Together
38

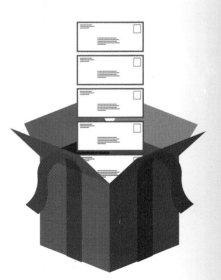

More than half of the personal computers used in business and education are connected to a network. The chances are good that you'll have to interact with a network soon if you don't already. This book helps you understand computer networks in several ways. It helps to scratch the intellectual itch you might have about where the data resides and what goes on inside the cable, equipment, and software. If you understand the basic structure and operation of a network, you can be more efficient in your job. The information in this book is an excellent foundation for growth if you want to learn more about networking. Finally, you can use this book as a training tool for working on networked computers.

Computer networking didn't just emerge as a unique and independent technology. Networking depends on many things you've seen or are familiar with already. In fact, modern networks have roots in the early telegraph and telephone systems. In this book, we take advantage of those historical ties to explain and illustrate the underlying technology of networks in a simple graphic format.

Then, we move into modern networking and explain the relationships between the hardware and software in networks. Our illustrations detail packets, network interface cards, servers, routers, management software, and many other aspects of networking. Our constant goal is to provide useful information in an easily understood manner.

The information in this book isn't specific to any particular type of computer or network operating system. We illustrate models of operation and tell you how some popular products fit into the models. If your computer is an IBM PC, DEC VAX, or an Apple Macintosh; if your network operating system is NetWare, LANtastic, or UNIX; and if your cabling is copper or fiber optic, the information in this book applies to your network.

# COMMUNICATION BY WIRE

CONTENTS

**W**E—BEING THE modern, up-to-the-minute kind of people computer users tend to be—like to think of networking as something new. Although the art and science of connecting computers via network cable are fairly new, the essential concepts used in computer networks are relatively old—nineteenth century old, as a matter of fact. The modern-day computer industry owes its existence to three Victorian-era inventions: the telegraph, telephone, and teletypewriter.

Samuel F. B. Morse (father of the telegraph and Morse code) wouldn't recognize a computer if you dropped one on his big toe, but he would recognize the logic and simplicity of ASCII, the essential modern-day computer alphabet and a descendant of Morse's telegraph code. Morse's original telegraph sent data (in the form of letters and numbers) from one place to another using a series of timed on-and-off pulses of electricity. Today's data communication systems still use on-and-off pulses of electricity to convey information—they just do it much faster than Morse ever imagined possible. In many ways, the telegraph was the first digital data communications system.

Alexander Graham Bell, also, wouldn't know what a modem is, but he would recognize the Victorian-era telephone-line interface that still connects most telephones and modems to the phone company's central office. The worldwide telephone system has changed rapidly over the years (largely due to the use of computers), but the *subscriber loop*—the wire between your home or office and the telephone company's equipment—hasn't changed much since Bell's day. The subscriber loop is an old-fashioned analog audio line. As we'll see, inventors over the years have gone to great lengths to connect digital computer systems to analog telephone lines.

Emile Baudot's invention didn't make his name a household word like Bell's and Morse's, but his multiplex printing telegraph was the forerunner of the computer printer and computer terminal. Other inventors improved and expanded on Baudot's ideas, and the teletypewriter was born. Before the invention of the computer, teletypewriters formed the basis of the Associated Press and United Press International news services. You may never have seen a teletypewriter, but you've probably heard its familiar *chunk-chunk-chunk* rhythm as the background noise on a radio or television newscast. Teletypewriters also form the basis of the worldwide TELEX network—a loosely bound network of machines that allows users to send printed messages to one another. (Although it was one of the most reliable of Teletype Corporation's machines, an ASR-33 Teletype machine played the part of the bad guy in the movie *Fail Safe*. The short version of the otherwise very complicated plot is that the United States and the former Soviet Union engage in nuclear warfare due to the failure of an ASR-33 at the American command headquarters. New York and Moscow are pulverized—all thanks to an errant scrap of paper stuck inside the machine.)

In the following three chapters, we'll show you how these three essential technologies converged to spark the beginning of the computer age.

# The Telegraph

ON MAY 24, 1844, American artist and inventor Samuel Morse sat at a desk in the Supreme Court chamber of the U.S. Capitol building in Washington, D.C., and sent his famous telegraph message—"What hath God wrought"—to a receiver 37 miles away in Baltimore. Morse had spent 12 years and every penny he owned to develop the telegraph.

To give credit where it is due, several other inventors in the United States and Europe also contributed to the development of the telegraph. Two English electrical pioneers, William Cooke and Charles Wheatstone, patented a telegraph in 1845. The Cooke-Wheatstone system was widely used by the British railroad system to relay traffic information between train stations.

The Cooke-Wheatstone telegraph used six wires and a delicate receiver mechanism with five magnetic needles. It was costly to build and cantankerous to operate. Morse's simpler telegraph used only one wire and a less complex, relatively rugged mechanism.

Fortunately for Morse, his telegraph was just what the young United States needed. America was expanding to the West, and Morse's telegraph followed the train tracks westward. Morse assigned his patents to the Magnetic Telegraph Company, and Magnetic signed up licensees to use the Morse patents. By 1851, there were 50 telegraph companies operating hundreds of telegraph offices—most of them located at railroad stations. You can still see old telegraph lines along the rail beds in many parts of the United States. In 1851, the Western Union Company was formed by the merger of 12 smaller telegraph companies. By 1866, Western Union boasted more than 4,000 offices nationwide, making it the world's first communications giant. By the turn of the century, Western Union operated over one million miles of telegraph lines, including two transatlantic cables.

The telegraph seems incredibly simple by today's standards, but it provided a much-needed link between the established business world of the Eastern United States and the sprawling frontier of the West. In one of those pleasant coincidences of history, it was just the right thing at just the right time.

# The Telegraph

The telegraph is basically an electromagnet connected to a battery via a switch. When the switch (the Morse key, or telegraph key) is down, current flows from the battery (at the sender's end of the line) through the key, down the wire, and into the sounder at the distant end of the line. By itself, the telegraph can express only two states, on or off. But by varying the timing and spacing of the on-and-off pulses, telegraph operators can send all the letters of the alphabet as well as numbers and punctuation marks. Morse code defines the timing and spacing of each character in terms of long and short "on" states called dashes and dots. For example, the letter A is dot-dash; the letter B is dash-dot-dot-dot.

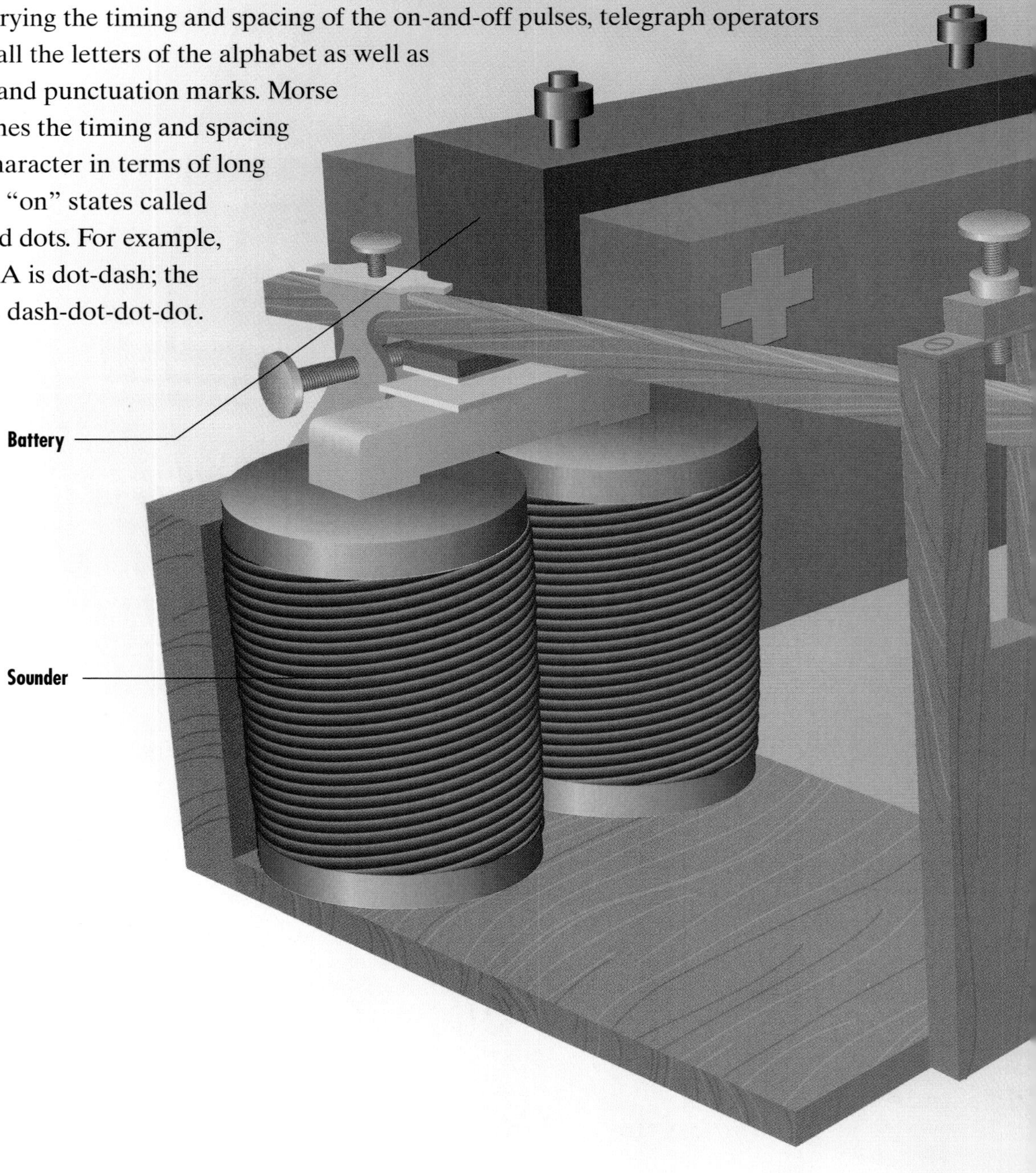

Battery

Sounder

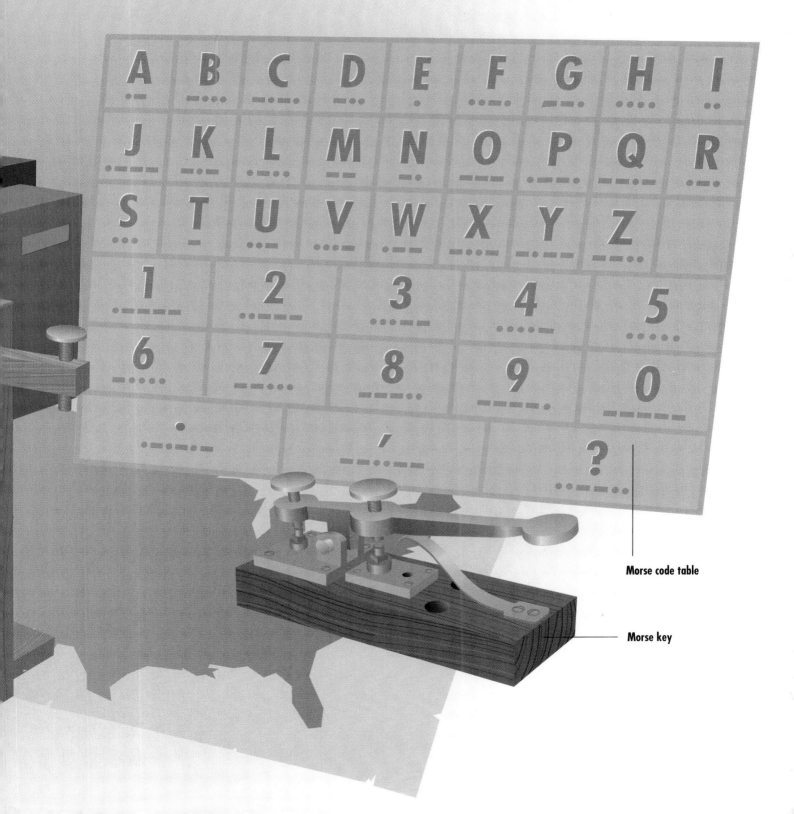

Morse code table

Morse key

# The Telegraph

### Morse's Port-Rule Telegraph

Morse's original telegraph used an automatic key to send messages and a printing mechanism to print the dots and dashes it received on a long strip of paper. To compose a message, the telegraph operator placed metal pieces in the notched stick, called a *port-rule*. To send the message, the operator placed the port-rule in the sender and turned the crank, moving the port-rule down the track. As the port-rule moved, it touched a metal contact, making or breaking the electrical connection.

At the receiving end, the current from the telegraph line moved an electromagnet up and down. A pencil attached to the magnet drew dots and dashes on a moving strip of paper; the paper was powered by a clock mechanism.

To read the message, the operator deciphered the dots and dashes and transcribed them by hand. Different combinations of dots and dashes represented different words, as defined in a master codebook. The limited number of possible combinations limited the number of words that could be sent. Morse later abandoned the printing mechanism when he discovered that telegraph operators could decipher the dots and dashes by ear.

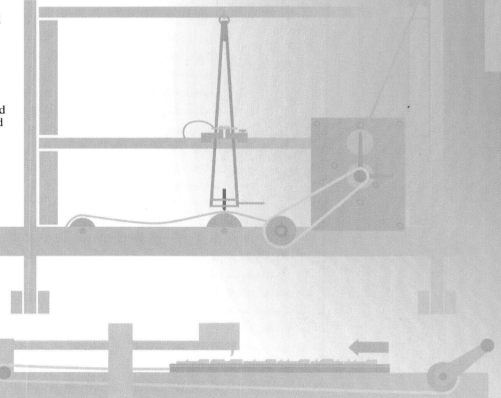

TO LIGHT THE ENTIRE CAPITOL AND THE SURROUNDING AREAS FOR ALMOST TEN MILES WHEN COMPLETE

### Edison's Printing Telegraph

Several famous inventors—including Alexander Bell and Thomas Edison—got their start in the telegraph industry. Edison, who worked as a telegraph operator in his youth, devised a printing telegraph that was used to relay stock-market information to investors. Rather than retaining patent rights, Edison often sold his patent rights to finance research in other areas.

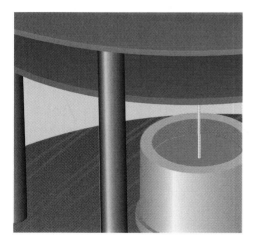

# The Telephone

ALEXANDER GRAHAM BELL invented the telephone, right? Well, right and wrong. Although Bell has received the lion's share of the credit, several other inventors also played major roles in the development of the telephone.

In 1861, German schoolteacher Phillip Reis created a device he called a telephone. Reis's device could transmit musical tones; had Reis spent more time refining the equipment, he might have succeeded in producing a viable voice telephone.

The two men who actually did invent the telephone did so under strikingly similar circumstances. Alexander Graham Bell of Boston and Elisha Gray of Chicago were both attempting to invent the *harmonic telegraph,* a device that would allow several telegraph signals to share one telegraph line (a problem later solved by no less an inventor than Thomas Edison). Neither inventor ever produced a working harmonic telegraph, and both men made the jump from telegraph to telephone at about the same time. Both men filed their patent papers with the U.S. Patent Office on the exact same day—February 14, 1876—but Bell arrived a few hours ahead of Gray.

The patent issued to Bell, U.S. Patent Number 174,465, is likely the most valuable patent ever issued. Bell and his backers immediately turned their attention from developing the telephone itself to perfecting and selling their invention.

The early years were not kind to Bell and company, and in early 1877 the Bell organization offered Western Union all rights to the Bell patents for $100,000. Western Union declined, setting off a series of encounters between the two companies that would finally culminate in AT&T's purchase of the remains of Western Union over a hundred years later.

Unimpressed with Bell's telephone, Western Union enlisted the services of Elisha Gray and Thomas Edison to design and market a technically superior telephone. Western Union was a giant corporation—the AT&T of its day—and had vast resources to spend on a legal battle. All the Bell Company had were its patents.

Western Union began to set up a telephone system to compete with Bell's. The Bell company filed suit. After two years of legal combat, Western Union's lawyers recommended that the company reach a settlement with Bell. The essential fact was that Bell had, indeed, beaten Gray to the patent office, and it was Bell and not Gray who held the basic telephone patents.

Under the terms of the agreement, Western Union surrendered its rights and patents in the telephone business to Bell. In addition, Western Union turned over its network of telephones to the Bell company in return for 20 percent of rental receipts for the life of the Bell patents.

The legal victory gave Bell a monopoly on the telephone business in the United States. One hundred years later, Bell's company (later known as AT&T) was the largest company in the world—larger than many national governments. Before the court-ordered dismantling of the AT&T empire in 1984, the company employed over one million people and operated over 100 million telephones.

Incidentally, the Reis telephone surfaced again years later, when several smaller telephone companies were attempting to nullify the Bell telephone patents. They hoped to use a Reis telephone as an example of "prior art," to prove that Bell's telephone was not the first successful design. But the judge in one case commented that "a century of Reis would never have produced a speaking telephone," and Bell went on to win virtually every patent lawsuit.

# Bell Liquid Telephone Transmitter

All telephones consist of a transmitter (the mouthpiece) and a receiver (the earpiece). To create a working telephone, Bell and the other inventors had to invent those two critical pieces.

Bell pursued two separate designs for the telephone transmitter. His first design used a membrane attached to a metal rod. The metal rod reached down into a cup of mild acid. As the user spoke downward into the microphone, the sound caused the membrane to move, which in turn moved the rod up and down in the cup of acid. As the rod moved up and down, the electrical resistance between the rod and the base of the cup varied.

There were several drawbacks to this variable-resistance, or liquid telephone, transmitter, not least of which was requiring the user to keep a supply of acid on hand. It was the acid, in fact, that caused Bell to utter the famous, "Mr. Watson, come here!" Bell had spilled the acid on his trousers.

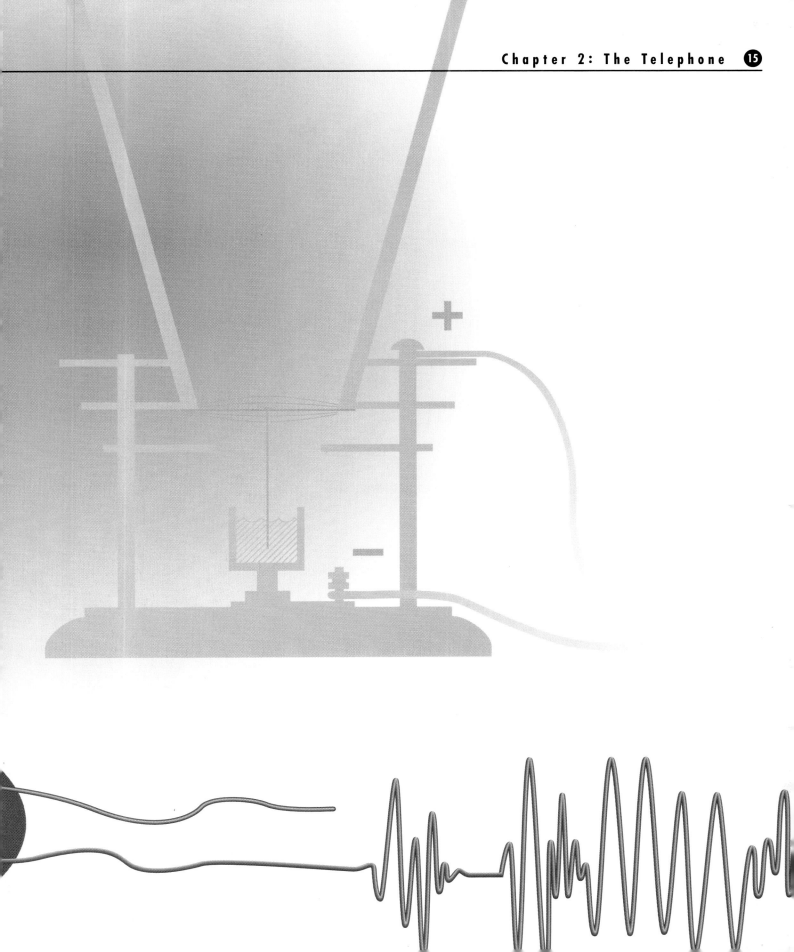

# Bell Induction Telephone Transmitter

Bell's second telephone transmitter used the principle of magnetic induction to change sound into electricity. Instead of a cup of acid, the induction transmitter used a membrane attached to a rod surrounded by a coil of wire. Sound striking the membrane moved the rod; as the rod moved back and forth inside the coil, it produced a weak electric current. The advantage of this device was that, theoretically, it could be used as both a transmitter and a receiver. But because the current it produced was very weak, it wasn't successful as a transmitter.

Despite its failure as a transmitter, the induction telephone worked very well as a receiver—so well, in fact, that most modern-day telephones and audio speakers still use a variation on Bell's original design.

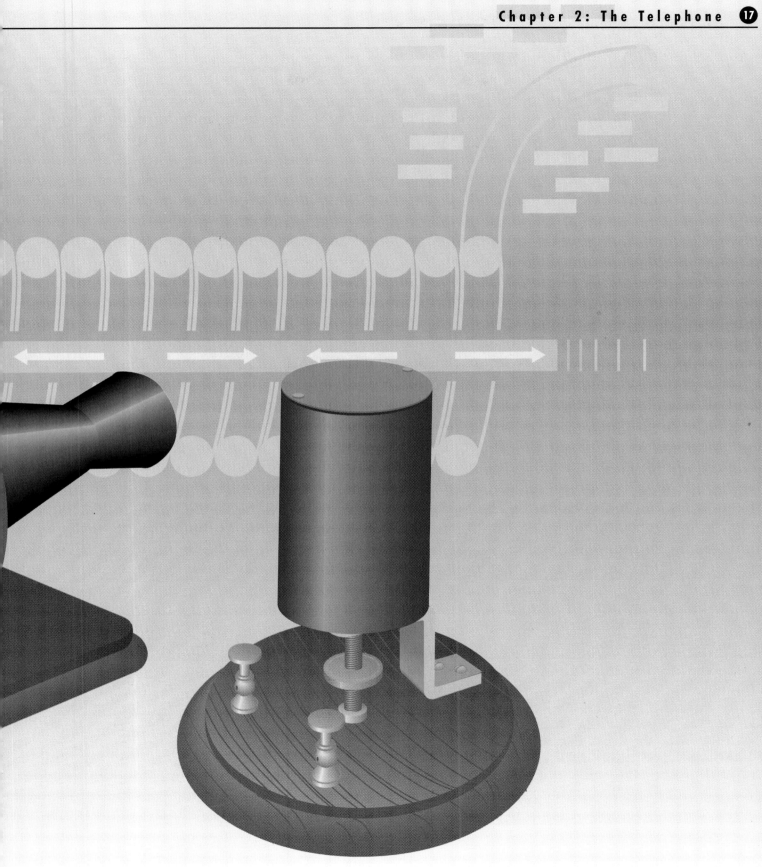

# Edison's Carbon Transmitter

The first truly practical telephone transmitter was designed by Thomas Edison, under contract for Western Union. Edison had discovered that certain carbon compounds change their electrical resistance when subjected to varying pressure. Edison sandwiched a carbon button between a metal membrane and a metal support. When sound struck the membrane, it exerted pressure on the carbon button, varying the flow of electricity through the microphone.

   Despite the hostilities between Bell and Western Union, the Bell people were quick to realize the superiority of Edison's design. When the *Bell v. Western Union* lawsuit was settled in 1879, Bell took over rights to Edison's transmitter. It became the standard telephone transmitter and is still in use today.

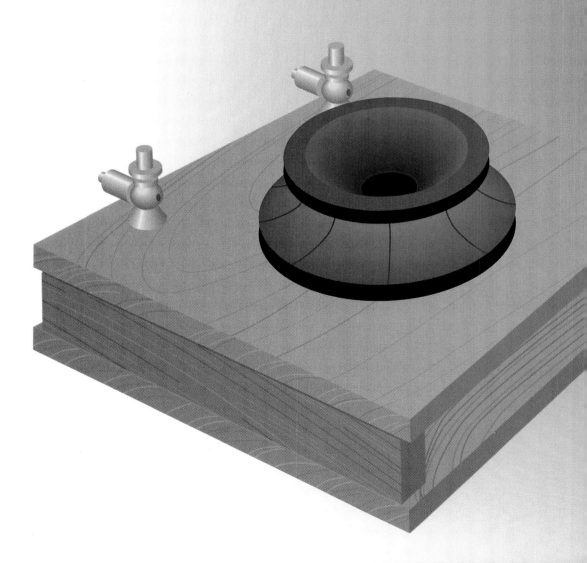

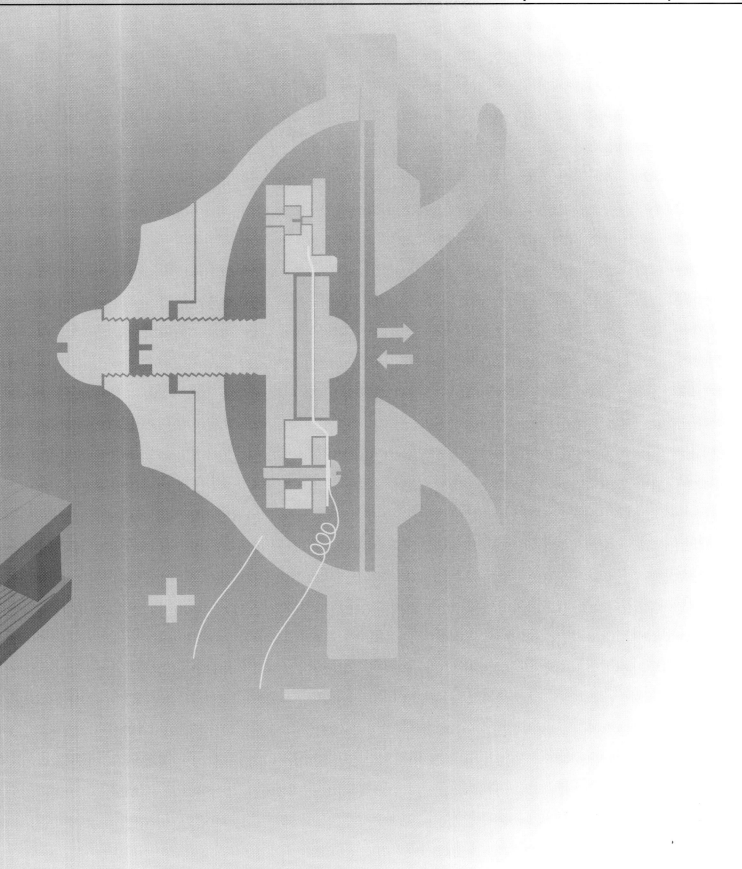

# Early Switchboard

The original telephone central offices were known as switchboards and were manually operated by a telephone operator. To make a call, you turned a crank on your telephone. The crank generated an electric current, which signaled the operator. To connect your phone to another, the operator inserted a plug into a jack corresponding to the desired phone.

In the central offices in small towns, the operators knew the correct jack for everyone in town. When you finished the call, the operator removed the plug, thus breaking the circuit. If the call was outside your local area, the operator used a trunk line to call another operator. The distant operator plugged the trunk line into the desired phone, and the call passed through.

Happy Birthday
Twin Brother!

Happy Birthday
Twin Brother!

# Strowger's Dial Telephone

As the telephone grew in popularity, the operator-and-switchboard approach became woefully inadequate. In 1889, a Kansas City undertaker named Almon Brown Strowger took the first step toward automating the phone system. His inventions, the Strowger switch and the telephone dial, allowed a caller to dial the desired number, eliminating the need for an operator.

# Two-Wire Circuit

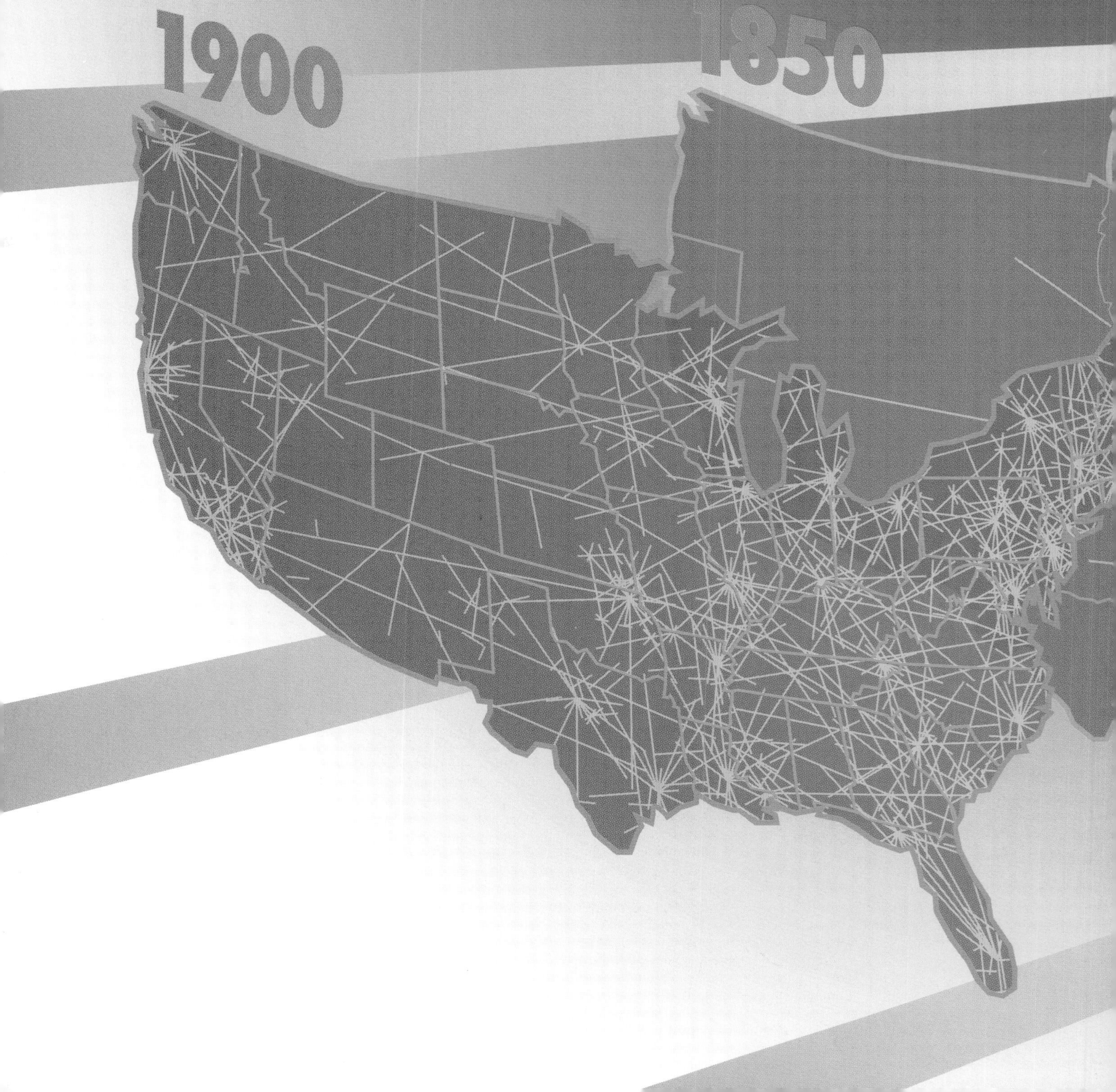

1900

1850

1800

Bell's original telephone used a single wire connection between telephones, with the earth itself providing the ground, or return, portion of the circuit. This approach saved on expensive wire, but left the telephone system very susceptible to interference from anything electrical. As the use of electricity spread, the amount of interference spread with it. By the mid-1880s, the Bell System and other telephone companies realized that the solution was to replace the one-wire telephone lines with two-wire circuits. This required the replacement of every telephone circuit in existence. Modern-day telephones still use the two-wire connection.

# CHAPTER 3

# Printing Telegraphs

**M**ORSE'S TELEGRAPH OPENED up the frontiers of electronic communications, but it had many shortcomings. First and foremost, the original Morse design allowed for only one conversation on the line at one time. Wire was handmade then, brittle, and very expensive. Installing the wire along the railroad tracks was time-consuming and often dangerous work. Several inventors, including Thomas Edison, put themselves to the task of inventing a multiplex telegraph—one that would allow several telegraph operators to use the same line at the same time. (Remember, Alexander Bell and Elisha Gray were both attempting to invent the harmonic telegraph—a form of multiplex telegraph—when they turned their attention to the telephone instead.)

Multiplexing made telegraph service more efficient and cost-effective, but a larger obstacle still remained: Morse's code itself. Sending messages via Morse code required a trained operator at each end of the wire. Western Union and its competitors were keen to develop a system that did not require constant human intervention.

As early as 1846 (only two years after Morse's first successful telegraph demonstration), a man with the unlikely name of Royal House invented a printing telegraph. Unfortunately, House's machine had its own set of problems. Although House claimed his machine was "twice as fast as Morse," it required two operators at each end of the line.

Several other inventors worked on printing telegraph machines, but French inventor Emile Baudot made many of the breakthroughs. Baudot's printing telegraph was the first to use a typewriterlike keyboard, and it allowed eight machines to share a single wire. More importantly, Baudot's machines did not use Morse code. Baudot's five-level code sent five pulses down the wire for each character transmitted. The machines themselves did the encoding and decoding, eliminating the need for operators to become proficient at Morse code. For the first time, electronic messages could be sent by nearly anyone.

English inventor Donald Murray expanded and improved on Baudot's work, and Murray sold the American rights to his inventions to Western Union and Western Electric. The Murray patents became the basis for the teletypewriter, also known by AT&T's brand name Teletype and by its generic nickname, TTY.

Western Union applied the new technology on its own network. Over time, the teletypewriter replaced the Morse key and sounder in most of Western Union's offices. Western Union also used the teletypewriter technology to provide a service called telex. Telex service allows subscribers to exchange typed messages with one another. Until the advent of the fax machine in the 1980s, telex service was widely used in international business.

AT&T operated a similar service called the Teletypewriter Exchange (TWX). Like telex, TWX service consisted of a teletypewriter connected to a dedicated phone line. TWX had the advantage of access to AT&T's wide-reaching telephone network. Like telex, TWX usage peaked in the 1960s and 1970s. In 1972, AT&T sold the TWX service to its old nemesis, Western Union.

In the 1930s and 1940s, several schemes were developed to allow the transmission of Teletype signals via shortwave radio. Radio Teletype, or RTTY, uses a technique called frequency shift keying (FSK) to simulate the on and off voltage used by conventional teletypes. In FSK, a signal on one frequency indicates ON, and a signal on the other indicates OFF. Since radio signals can be keyed on and off very quickly, RTTY signals run at speeds similar to land-line teletypewriters.

RTTY signals broadcast via shortwave radio allow many stations to receive the same signal. RTTY was widely used by United Press International (UPI) and the Associated Press (AP) wire services before cheaper, more reliable satellite links became available in the 1980s. RTTY in various forms is still used today for ship-to-shore telex service and for marine and aeronautical weather information.

# The Teletypewriter

For fifty years after its invention at the turn of the century, the teletypewriter was the mainstay of nonvoice electronic communications. Teletypewriters were frequently connected in a round-robin circuit. In this configuration, the original signal is sent from one point on the circuit and received by all the other machines on the circuit. This type of circuit was widely used by news wire services such as the Associated Press and United Press International.

New York (AP) The President announced t...

...cessful agreement by all partie...

The President announced today the successful agreement by all parties to an International Free Trade and Business Act. Seven countries endorsed the plan, including the United

Seven countries endorse

International Free Trade

and Business Act.

Unlike the Baudot code, Morse code uses characters of unequal length and size. For example the letter E is expressed as one dot, but the number 0 is expressed as five dashes. This inequality of size makes Morse easy to detect by ear but very difficult to decode mechanically.

The Baudot code uses five equal-length elements (Morse would have called them "dots") to define each character of the alphabet. Five elements can define only $2^5$, or 32, different combinations—not enough to print the entire alphabet plus numerals and punctuation marks. To overcome this problem, two special nonprinting characters, called Figs and Ltrs, shift the printing mechanism between letters (A–Z) mode and figures (numbers and punctuation marks) mode. The two modes allow the code to represent a total of 62 characters.

## BAUDOT
### CODE SIGNALS
red denotes positive current

| start | 1 | 2 | 3 | 4 | 5 | stop | LETTERS shift | FIGURES |
|-------|---|---|---|---|---|------|---------------|---------|
| | | | | | | | A | - |
| | | | | | | | B | ? |
| | | | | | | | C | : |
| | | | | | | | D | $ |
| | | | | | | | E | 3 |
| | | | | | | | F | ! |
| | | | | | | | G | & |
| | | | | | | | H | # |
| | | | | | | | I | 8 |
| | | | | | | | J | bell |
| | | | | | | | K | ( |
| | | | | | | | L | |
| | | | | | | | M | |

CHAPTER

4

# The Early Networks

**W**HEN YOU HEAR the word *network* today, you probably think of computer networks, television networks, cable television networks, or local area networks. All of those networks owe their existence to two earlier networks: Western Union's network and the Bell system.

Western Union's network was the first to span the North American continent. Following the railroad westward, Western Union struck deals with most of the railroads of the day. In exchange for access to the railroad right-of-way, Western Union provided a telegraph station and an operator at each train station. The operator handled schedule and load information for the railroad at no charge.

Western Union's service was point-to-point. To send a telegram to someone, you would go to the Western Union office and dictate the message to the telegraph operator. The operator would then send the message out in Morse code over the telegraph line to the appropriate station.

When Bell Telephone began operations in the late 1890s, it had no telephone lines. As subscribers signed up for service, Bell ran new lines to the subcribers' locations. Initially, telephone service was also point-to-point, meaning that each phone could connect to only one other phone. Many of the early telephone subscribers were doctors; they would connect one phone in an office to another at home. As telephone service grew, subscribers wanted to be able to talk to one another— so the telephone network, as we know it today, was born.

Today's public telephone network is a complex maze of telephone lines and central switching offices. The central offices connect to an even more complicated web of cables, microwave towers, fiber optic cables, and communications satellites.

At one time, more than 90 percent of these facilities belonged to the Bell system. Since the court-ordered AT&T breakup in 1984, the facilities belong to dozens of companies, including AT&T, the regional Bell operating companies, MCI, GTE, and others. Despite all the behind-the-scenes complexity, the system remains easy to use. To make a call, you simply pick up the phone and dial the number.

# Western Union's Network

Western Union holds a special place in history: It was the world's first telecommunications giant. The completion of its first overland telegraph line ended the brief, exciting history—1860 to 1861—of the colorful pony express. Western Union was formed by the merger of 12 smaller companies. By the time of the Civil War, Western Union's lines stretched across the United States, from New York to California.

# The Telephone Network

**1** The early telephone network was built using iron or copper wire hung from wooden poles. Each telephone required its own two-wire pair to connect the telephone to the phone company's equipment. As the number of telephones exploded, so did the number of telephone wires. Today, many telephones are still connected to a central office using a two-wire connection that Alexander Bell would recognize.

**2** All telephones are connected to a central office. In many cases, fiber optic cables, microwave radio, and satellite dishes have replaced the traditional copper wire. The central office connects calls between subscribers in the same central office and routes calls to other central offices or long-distance facilities.

PBX

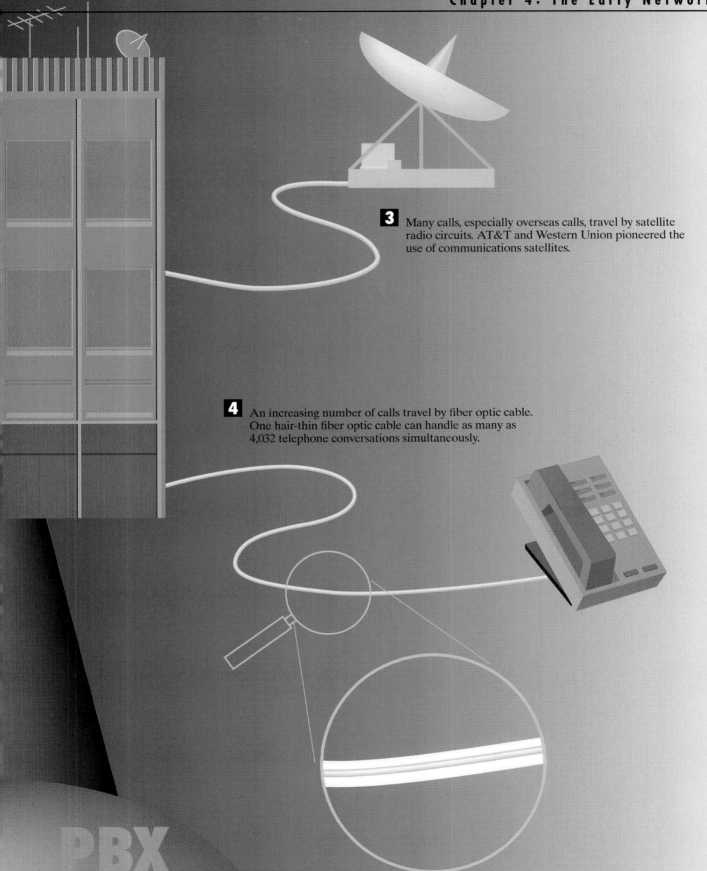

**3** Many calls, especially overseas calls, travel by satellite radio circuits. AT&T and Western Union pioneered the use of communications satellites.

**4** An increasing number of calls travel by fiber optic cable. One hair-thin fiber optic cable can handle as many as 4,032 telephone conversations simultaneously.

PBX

# 2

# COMPUTERS
# AND TELEPHONES
# TOGETHER

CONTENTS

OVERVIEW

**A**LTHOUGH THEY ARE products of different eras and different technologies, the computer and the telephone seem to have been made for one another. Today's telephone network could not exist without vast computing resources to process calls, route traffic, and print telephone bills. Conversely, the existence of a worldwide telephone network allows computers to connect to one another so that the machines (and their users) may exchange information.

Even though the computer and the telephone have been forced into a marriage of convenience, they are worlds apart. The computer's universe is digital: Everything that passes through the computer's CPU is either a 1 or a 0. The worldwide telephone network is largely digital, too—except for the last few miles of wire between the customer's home or office and the telephone company's switching equipment. In order to maintain compatibility with the millions of existing telephones, the local loop from the telephone company central office to the phone jack on your wall is the same two-wire circuit used by the Bell system since the 1890s.

AT&T was one of the first companies to adopt computers on a very large scale, and AT&T, through its Bell Labs subsidiary, funded some of the earliest computer research. The invention of the transistor at Bell Labs in 1948 made large-scale computers practical. AT&T also invented the first practical telephone modem—a device that allows digital data to travel via the analog world of the telephone network.

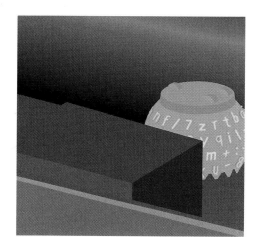

# From Keypunches to Terminals

**A**S WE WRITE this chapter, we're sitting in front of a 17-inch color screen with 1024 by 768 pixel resolution in 256 colors. The keyboard has 103 keys, many of them reserved for special functions such as moving paragraphs or underlining a passage of text. As we type, our keystrokes instantly appear on the color screen, the text formatted and displayed exactly as it will appear when this page is printed. The printer can faithfully reproduce 35 different typefaces with 600 dot-per-inch accuracy.

But the earliest computers didn't have any of these features—in fact, they didn't even have a keyboard and screen. The very first computers used a variety of input and output devices, including switches, lights, teletypewriters, and paper-tape readers.

Because early computers were used primarily by scientists for one specific task, there was no pressing need to make data input and output faster or easier. But when computers became available and affordable for general business use, efficiency and accessibility became important concerns.

The first input/output device to find widespread acceptance was the keypunch and card reader combination. Data to be input to the computer was typed into a keypunch machine. The machine translated the operator's keystrokes into a series of holes punched in a card. The cards were then carried to the computer room, where they were placed into a card reader. The card reader "sensed" the holes in the cards and recreated the operator's keystrokes.

The punched-card system had many drawbacks: It was cumbersome, the cards could easily get out of order, and the input/output cycle took time—sometimes days or weeks. The punched-card system also had advantages: The keypunch machines could be located anywhere, and card decks from multiple locations could be sent to one central location for processing. Keypunch operators didn't require extensive training, since the keypunch keyboard resembled a standard typewriter keyboard. But the biggest disadvantage of the punched-card system was that it allowed only one program to run on the computer at one time.

The next step forward in the human-machine interface was the interactive printing terminal. Instead of punching holes in a card, the terminal sent keystrokes directly to the computer. The computer responded by sending characters to the terminal's printer. The early interactive terminals were usually teletypewriters or specially modified electric typewriters. With the advent of the time-sharing operating system, several operators could run jobs on the same computer at the same time. These machines were cantankerous and noisy, but they provided an immediate response from the computer—something the punched-card system could never do. The ability to get immediate answers from the computer led to a host of new applications for computer technology.

Perhaps the most significant of these new applications was the on-line processing system like those used in airline reservation systems. Using special leased telephone lines, airlines could place terminals in every city they served. Ticket agents across the country could use the central computer system to check fares and book flights. The on-line processing concept was and still is used in many other industries, including the computer industry itself.

Before the interactive terminal, programmers had to develop computer programs using punched cards. The delays and additional errors introduced by the punched-card system made an already difficult job even more difficult. The interactive terminal allowed programmers to see the results of their work immediately, thus reducing the amount of time required to develop a program.

Although the interactive printing terminal added a lot to the world of computing, it also left a great deal to be desired. Printing terminals are, by nature, mechanical devices. Even though they're faster than punched cards, they're still relatively slow, noisy, and require a great deal of maintenance.

In the mid-1960s, several manufacturers began to replace the terminal's printing mechanism with a picture tube, and the video display terminal (VDT) was born. VDTs work much like printing terminals do, but they are faster, quieter, and more efficient. The earliest microcomputer systems—the immediate predecessors to today's personal computers—also used VDTs for input and output.

# Punched Card

The punched card was the primary means of data input and output for many years. The card itself was made of heavy paper and could store 80 characters of information—one in each column. The card and method of coding date back to a mechanical vote-counting machine invented by Herman Hollerith in 1890.

80 CHARACTERS PER CARD

```
0 0 0 0 0 0 0 0 0 0 0 0 0 0 0 0 0 0 0 0 0 0 0 0 0 0 0 0 0 0 0 0 0 0 0
45 46 47 48 49 50 51 52 53 54 55 56 57 58 59 60 61 62 63 64 65 66 67 68 69 70 71 72 73 74 75 76 77 78 79 80
1 1 1 1 1 1 1 1 1 1 1 1 1 1 1 1 1 1 1 1 1 1 1 1 1 1 1 1 1 1 1 1 1 1 1 1
2 2 2 2 2 2 2 2 2 2 2 2 2 2 2 2 2 2 2 2 2 2 2 2 2 2 2 2 2 2 2 2 2 2 2 2
3 3 3 3 3 3 3 3 3 3 3 3 3 3 3 3 3 3 3 3 3 3 3 3 3 3 3 3 3 3 3 3 3 3 3 3
4 4 4 4 4 4 4 4 4 4 4 4 4 4 4 4 4 4 4 4 4 4 4 4 4 4 4 4 4 4 4 4 4 4 4 4
5 5 5 5 5 5 5 5 5 5 5 5 5 5 5 5 5 5 5 5 5 5 5 5 5 5 5 5 5 5 5 5 5 5
6 6 6 6 6 6 6 6 6 6 6 6 6 6 6 6 6 6 6 6 6 6 6 6 6 6 6 6 6 6 6 6 6
7 7 7 7 7 7 7 7 7 7 7 7 7 7 7 7 7 7 7 7 7 7 7 7 7 7 7 7 7
8 8 8 8 8 8 8 8 8 8 8 8 8 8 8 8 8 8 8 8 8 8 8 8 8 8 8 8
9 9 9 9 9 9 9 9 9 9 9 9 9 9 9 9 9 9 9 9 9 9 9 9 9 9 9 9 9 9 9 9 9 9 9
45 46 47 48 49 50 51 52 53 54 55 56 57 58 59 60 61 62 63 64 65 66 67 68 69 70 71 72 73 74 75 76 77 78 79 80
```

A typical 230 MB hard-disk drive
stores the equivalent of a stack
of punch cards almost half a mile
tall—more than twice the height
of the Empire State Building!

# IBM Selectric Terminal

The IBM Selectric printing terminal was the first interactive printing terminal designed specifically for use on a computer system. Earlier printing terminals were derived from teletypewriters, but the Selectric machine was a completely new design.

The Selectric introduced IBM's now-famous golf ball rotating-type element. Although the Selectric was more reliable and created more attractive type than its predecessors did, it wasn't any quieter.

# Early Video Display Terminal

The Lear-Siegler ADM-3A terminal shown here wasn't the first video terminal, but it was one of the most popular. The ADM-3A could display 24 lines of 80 characters each.

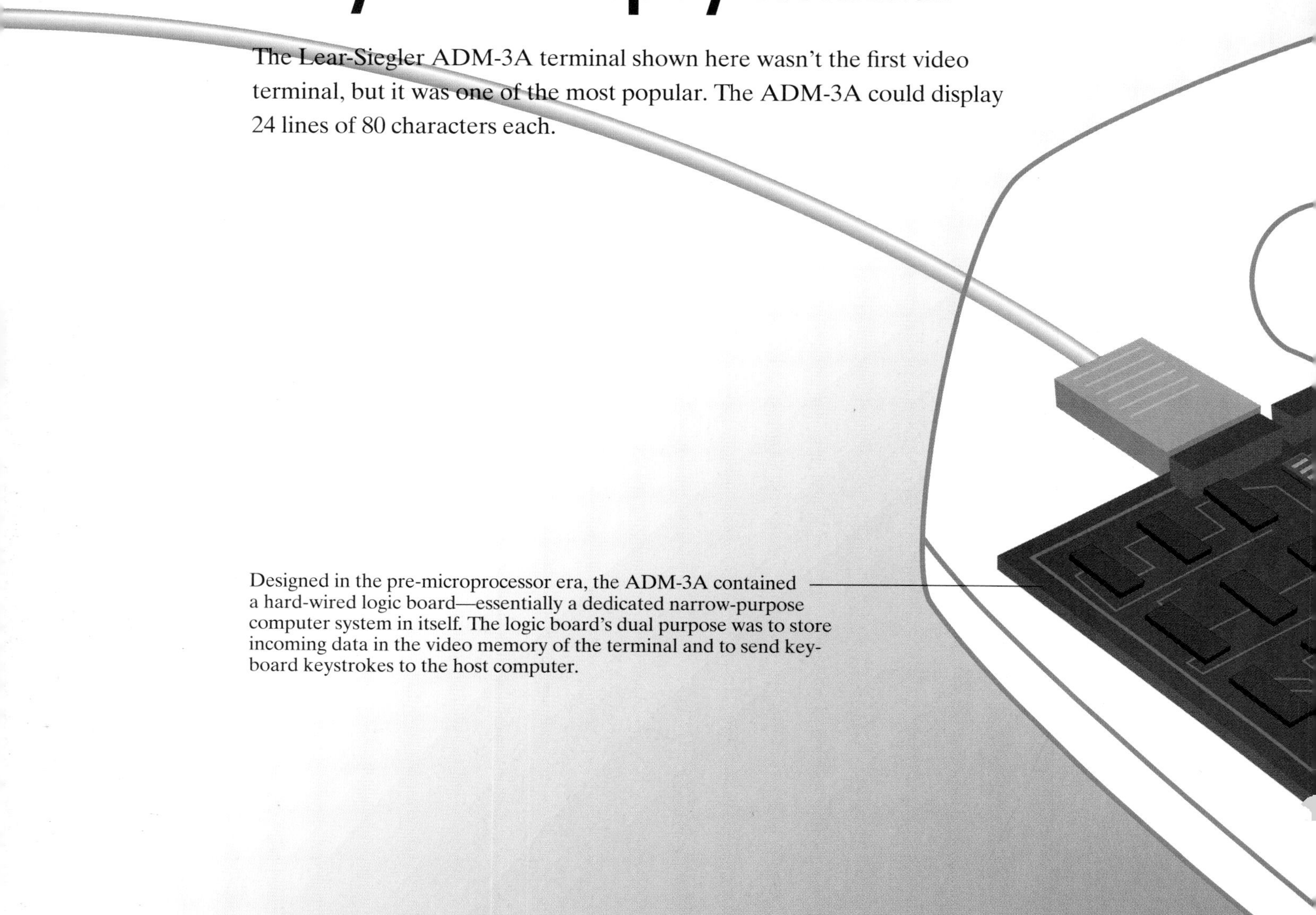

Designed in the pre-microprocessor era, the ADM-3A contained a hard-wired logic board—essentially a dedicated narrow-purpose computer system in itself. The logic board's dual purpose was to store incoming data in the video memory of the terminal and to send keyboard keystrokes to the host computer.

Because so many computer operators were accustomed to teletypewriter keyboards, most early VDT keyboards followed teletypewriter conventions for placement of the punctuation and special characters. Early Apple computers also used this layout.

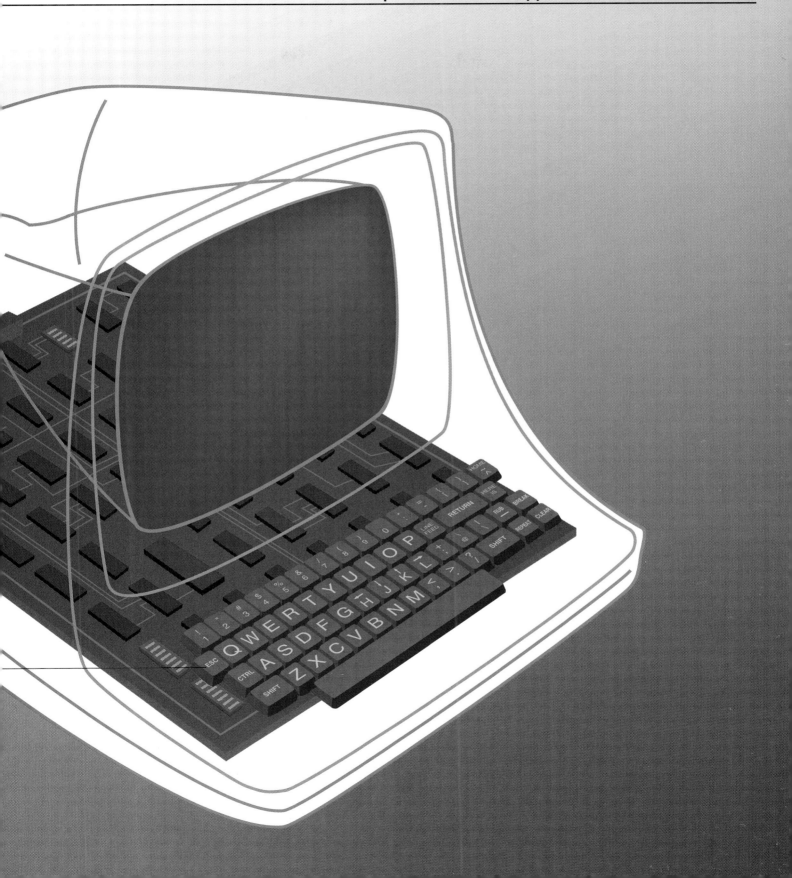

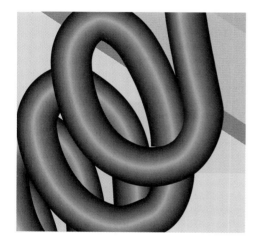

# The Carterfone

N 1966, a small Texas company called Carterfone invented a simple device that allowed mobile two-way radios to connect to a telephone line. The Carterfone allowed construction workers, field service personnel, and traveling executives to make and receive telephone calls via their company's existing two-way radio system.

The Carterfone did not physically connect to the phone line. Nevertheless, AT&T maintained that the Carterfone posed a threat to the integrity of the telephone system. After a two-year battle, the FCC ruled that third-party equipment could indeed be connected to the telephone network as long as the connected device contained protective measures to ensure that no harm could come to the telephone network. The Carterfone decision was the beginning of the end of AT&T's near-monopoly on telephones and telephone-related equipment.

In 1975, the FCC went a step further. The FCC ruled that any piece of equipment could be attached to the telephone company's lines, if the device met certain technical specifications. In 1977, the FCC published these technical specifications, known as Rules and Regulations of the Federal Communications Commission, Part 68: Connection of Terminal Equipment to the Telephone Network. The rules, commonly known as Part 68, describe how third-party equipment should connect to the telephone network. If you look on the bottom of almost any telephone or modem sold in the United States today, you'll see a sticker stating that the device conforms to Part 68 of the FCC rules.

The FCC's Part 68 rules opened a floodgate of new equipment. Dozens of manufacturers jumped into the telephone business. Instead of paying a few dollars every month to the local phone company, you could buy a phone of your own. Telephones became available in every imaginable shape, size, and color. Telephone accessories such as answering machines, cordless phones, and modems became common household items. The telephone industry itself was turned upside down, all thanks to a little company from Texas.

# The Carterfone

It may not look like much, but this simple device turned AT&T's equipment business upside down. Because the Carterfone engineers weren't allowed to connect their equipment directly to the Bell system lines, they chose a method called acoustic coupling to pass sound between the two-way radio and the telephone line.

The top portion of the Carterfone is made
of molded plastic. When a radio user needed
a telephone connection, the radio operator at
the base station placed a telephone handset into the
Carterfone and dialed the call. Inside the Carterfone,
an induction microphone picks up sound from the telephone receiver, and a miniature speaker talks into the
telephone microphone.

C H A P T E R

# Alphabet Soup: Morse, Baudot, ASCII, and EBCDIC

LIKE MORSE CODE before it, Emile Baudot's five-level teletypewriter code introduced the world to a faster, more efficient form of communications. Baudot's code, with improvements and additions made by English inventor Donald Murray, served as the primary code used in machine-to-machine communications for over fifty years. But despite its longevity, the Baudot code had several shortcomings.

As we saw in Chapter 3, the Baudot code uses 5 bits of data to represent each transmitted character. A special shift code is used to shift the receiving machine between letters and figures mode. Even with the shift code, the Baudot code can only accommodate uppercase letters.

In 1966, several American computer, teletypewriter, and communications companies collaborated to devise a replacement for the Baudot code. The result of their work is the American Standard Code for Information Interchange, or *ASCII*. ASCII uses a 7-bit code, allowing it to represent 128 discrete characters without using a shift code. ASCII defines 96 printable characters (the letters *A* through *Z* in upper- and lowercase, numbers *0* through *9*, and punctuation marks) and also includes several control characters that define nonprinting functions such as carriage return, line feed, and backspace.

Besides offering full upper- and lowercase printing, ASCII also defines a simple error-checking mechanism. An extra bit, called the parity bit, is added to each transmitted character. If the communications circuit is using even parity, then the parity bit is set to 1 when there is an even number of bits in the transmitted character. If the circuit is using odd parity, the parity bit is set to 1 when there is an odd number of bits. Although parity checking doesn't provide a means to retransmit corrupted characters, it does provide a simple validity test for received data.

ASCII was widely and readily adopted by most computer and communications equipment vendors worldwide (IBM was the notable exception). Beyond the improvements ASCII offered over Baudot, ASCII provided a well-defined public standard that didn't owe its existence to any one company. As an added bonus, any ASCII-standard computer could, at least in theory, exchange information with any other ASCII system.

IBM, following a long-standing tradition of doing things its own way, did not adopt ASCII. Instead, IBM engineers devised their own code, called EBCDIC, for Extended Binary Coded Decimal Interchange Code. EBCDIC is an 8-bit code, so it can define a total of 256 different characters. This is its one advantage over ASCII. Unlike ASCII, the alphabetic characters in EBCDIC are not sequential, making sorting operations more difficult.

Although it is still widely used in IBM mainframes and minicomputers, EBCDIC never caught on in the non-IBM universe. IBM itself has shunned EBCDIC on several occasions, most notably in the design of the IBM Personal Computer and PS/2 machines, which both use ASCII, but with a twist. The ASCII character set implemented in the IBM PC and compatible machines is what IBM calls Extended ASCII. Like EBCDIC, it uses 8 bits to allow for 256 possible characters. The lower 128 characters (values 0 through 127) are standard ASCII, and the higher 128 characters contain characters for drawing boxes and lines, international punctuation and diacritical marks, and scientific notation characters.

# From Morse Code to EBCDIC

Because Morse code was meant for human ears, it contains data elements of unequal length. The dash is three times the length of the dot, and a period equal to one dot is added between letters, so the receiving operator can discern one letter from the next.

The five data elements of Baudot code (called "bits" today) are of equal length to define each character. Because 5 bits allow only 32 combinations, Baudot code uses two special characters called FIGS and LTRS to tell the receiving machine to print the figures character set or the letters set. This effectively doubles the number of code combinations to 64. Baudot code is uppercase only, and the characters are not in sequential numerical order: For example, *A* has a value of 24, *B* is 19, and *C* is 14.

ASCII improves on Baudot code in several key ways. The use of 7 data elements, or bits, allows ASCII to represent up to 128 discrete characters: 31 characters are reserved for such special functions as carriage return, backspace, and line feed, and 96 characters are reserved for the letters *A* through *Z* in upper- and lowercase, as well as numbers and punctuation marks. ASCII characters are in sequential order: *A* is 65, *B* is 66, *C* is 67, and so on. This facilitates computer manipulation of ASCII text and numbers.

IBM's EBCDIC uses 8 data bits, allowing it to represent 256 discrete characters and symbols, of which 63 characters are reserved for control functions. In this table, *A* is 193, *B* is 194, *C* is 195. However, EBCDIC is not sequential: Its character set—unlike ASCII's—does not follow sequential order. There are gaps between *i* and *j* and again between *r* and *s*.

**MORSE**

**BAUDOT**

16 8 4 2 1

$16 + 8 = 24$

**ASCII**

64 32 16 8 4 2 1

$64 + 1 = 65$

**EBCDIC**

128 64 32 16 8 4 2 1

$128 + 64 + 1 = 193$

● = ON BITS      ○ = OFF BITS

# B C

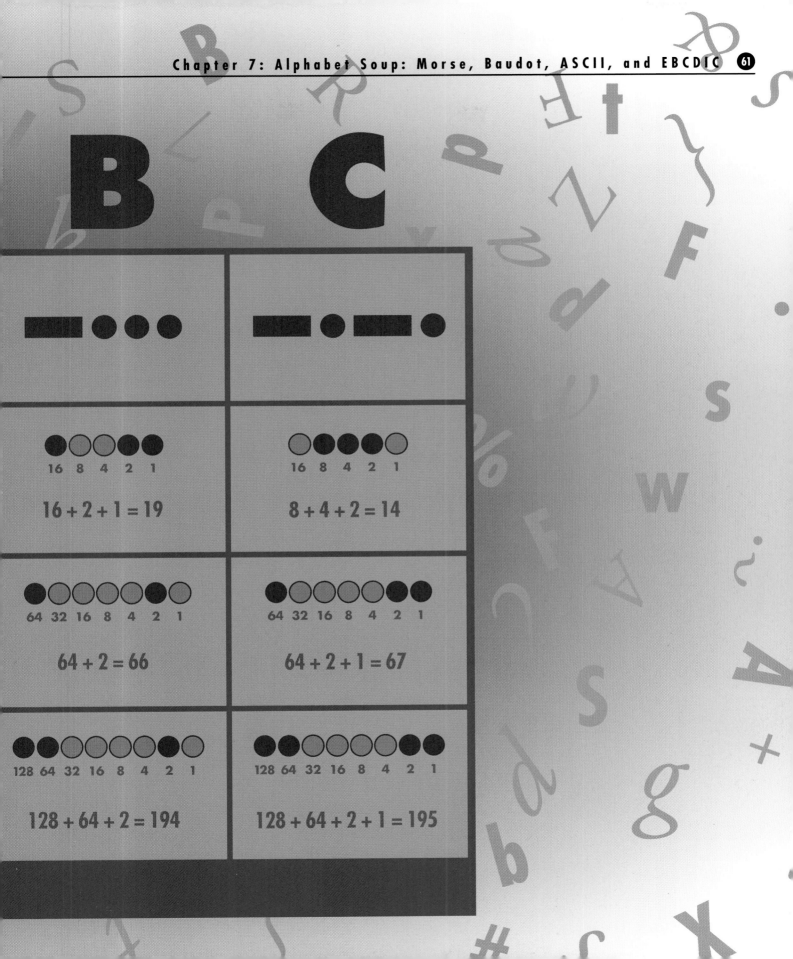

$16 + 2 + 1 = 19$

$8 + 4 + 2 = 14$

64 32 16 8 4 2 1

64 32 16 8 4 2 1

$64 + 2 = 66$

$64 + 2 + 1 = 67$

128 64 32 16 8 4 2 1

128 64 32 16 8 4 2 1

$128 + 64 + 2 = 194$

$128 + 64 + 2 + 1 = 195$

# The RS-232C Serial Interface

THE EARLIEST ELECTRONIC communications devices—the telegraph and teletypewriter—communicated by switching on and off voltage on a wire. The voltage used varied according to the equipment in use and the length of the wire involved. The circuit between two machines typically allowed communication in one direction at a time.

Today's high-speed data communications equipment still operates on the principle of switching voltage on and off, but many improvements have been made to the basic communications circuit. In an attempt to ensure that one serial device will talk to another, the Electronics Industries Association (EIA) created a standard to define the electrical signaling and cable connection characteristics of a serial port. In 1969, the EIA established Recommended Standard (RS) number 232 in version C, or RS-232C, the most common type of communications circuit in use today.

The ASCII character set defines what numbers to use for each character, and the RS-232C standard defines a way to move the data over a communications link. Commonly used with ASCII characters, RS-232C may also be used to transmit Baudot or EBCDIC data.

The RS-232C standard defines the function of the signals in the serial interface as well as the physical connection used by the interface. This standard defines two classes of serial connections: one for terminals, or *DTE* (Data Terminal Equipment), and one for communications equipment, or *DCE* (Data Communications Equipment). A DTE device usually connects to a DCE device. For example, a personal computer (DTE) can connect to a modem (DCE). The serial port on most personal computers is configured as a DTE port.

An RS-232C connection normally uses a 25-pin D-shell connector with a male plug on the DTE end and a female plug on the DCE end. Rules (and EIA standards) were made to be broken, and many manufacturers have taken liberties with the hardware they use to implement the RS-232C standard. When the IBM PC/AT first appeared in 1984, IBM decided to use a 9-pin connector for the serial port. The AT's serial port shares an expansion card with a parallel printer port. There isn't enough room on the card bracket for two 25-pin plugs, so IBM abbreviated the serial connector to a 9-pin plug. Other manufacturers followed suit, so you may encounter either type of connector on your desktop computer, and you'll certainly find 9-pin connectors on laptop and notebook computers. Some manufacturers provide both 9-pin and 25-pin connectors for the same serial port.

# The RS-232C Serial Interface

An RS-232C serial connection consists of several independent circuits sharing the same cable and connector. There are two data circuits (send and receive), and there are several control circuits, called handshaking lines, which control the flow of data between the terminal and the host.

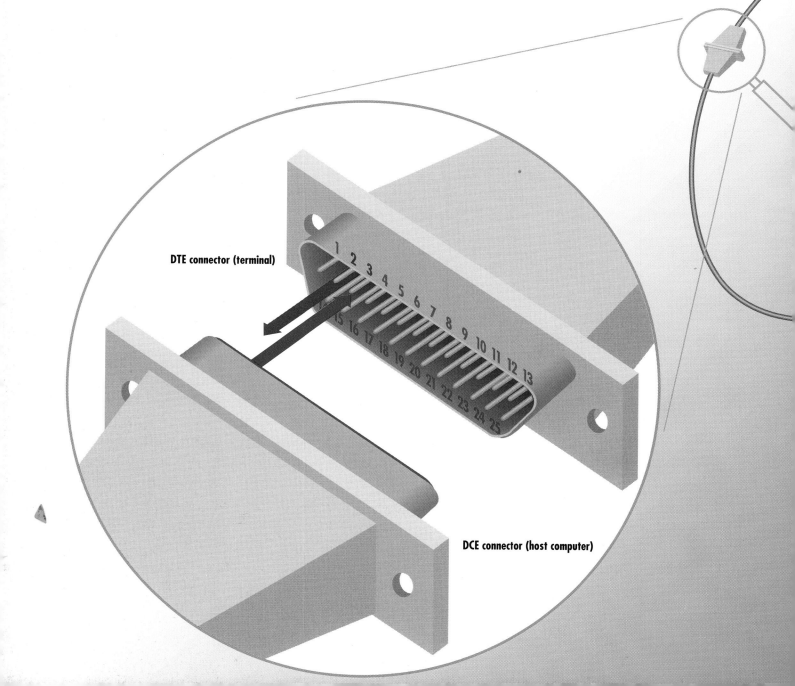

DTE connector (terminal)

DCE connector (host computer)

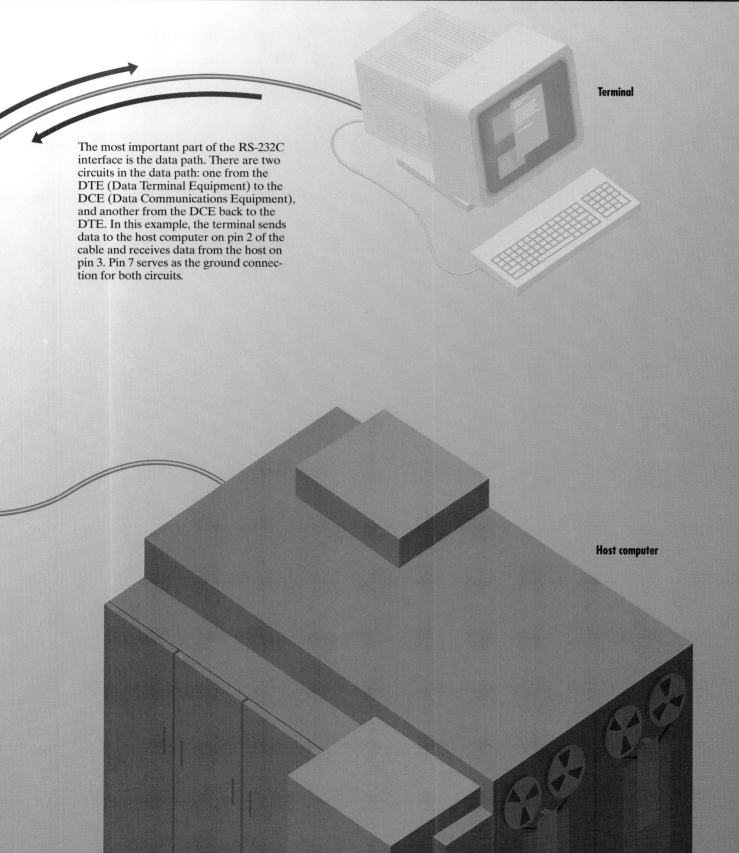

Terminal

The most important part of the RS-232C interface is the data path. There are two circuits in the data path: one from the DTE (Data Terminal Equipment) to the DCE (Data Communications Equipment), and another from the DCE back to the DTE. In this example, the terminal sends data to the host computer on pin 2 of the cable and receives data from the host on pin 3. Pin 7 serves as the ground connection for both circuits.

Host computer

# The Bell 103 Modem

**T**HE EARLY ELECTRONIC communications devices—the telegraph and teletypewriter—communicated with one another by exchanging pulsed direct current (DC) signals over a long wire. Modern-day computers and terminals use an improved version of this technique, as defined by the RS-232C and other computer communications standards.

Telephones, in contrast, communicate by passing an analog audio signal over the line. The strength and frequency of the signal varies depending on the volume and pitch of the sound being sent. Because the telephone network is designed to carry voice signals, it cannot carry the DC signals used in computer communications.

As the use of computers spread in the late 1950s and early 1960s, a need arose to connect computers and terminals via ordinary telephone lines. AT&T's answer was the Bell 103 modem. A modem (that is, a *mod*ulator/*dem*odulator) converts the on-and-off digital pulses of computer data into on-and-off analog tones that can be transmitted over a normal telephone circuit.

The Bell 103 modem operates at a speed of 300 bits per second. This is painfully slow by modern-day standards, but it was fast enough for the slow-printing terminals of the day. Because it allowed the terminal to be physically separated from the host computer, the modem made computing resources available from virtually anyplace.

Recent improvements in modem technology allow speeds up to 57,600 bits per second, 192 times the speed of the original Bell 103 modem. As we'll see in Chapter 12, these modems use microprocessors to achieve these high communications speeds. Ironically, some newer modems contain more computing power than many early mainframe computer systems!

Regardless of the communications speed, all modems share some common characteristics. Since they must connect to a computer or terminal, virtually all modems contain an RS-232C communications interface. Similarly, most modems also contain an RJ-11 telephone-line interface—the familiar clear plastic four-wire telephone plug.

The Bell 103 modem uses two pairs of tones to represent the on-and-off states of the RS-232C data line. One pair of tones is used by the modem originating the call, and the other pair is used by the modem answering the call. The modem sends data by switching between the two tones in each pair. The calling modem sends data by switching between 1,070 and 1,270 hertz, and the answering modem sends data by switching between 2,025 and 2,225 hertz.

Newer modems use more and different tones to convey information, but the basic principle remains the same.

# A Modem Connection

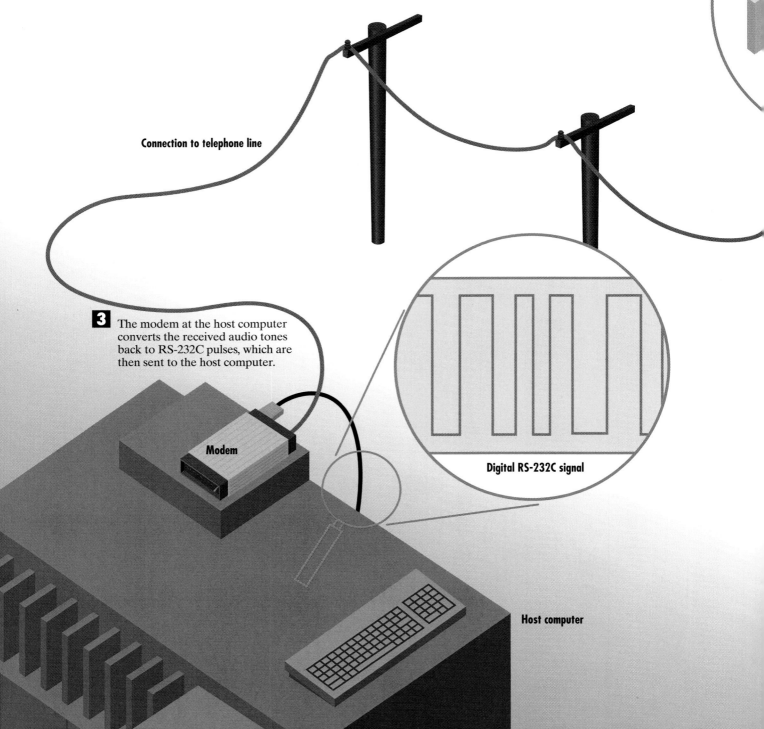

RS-232C connection to terminal

Connection to telephone line

**3** The modem at the host computer converts the received audio tones back to RS-232C pulses, which are then sent to the host computer.

Modem

Digital RS-232C signal

Host computer

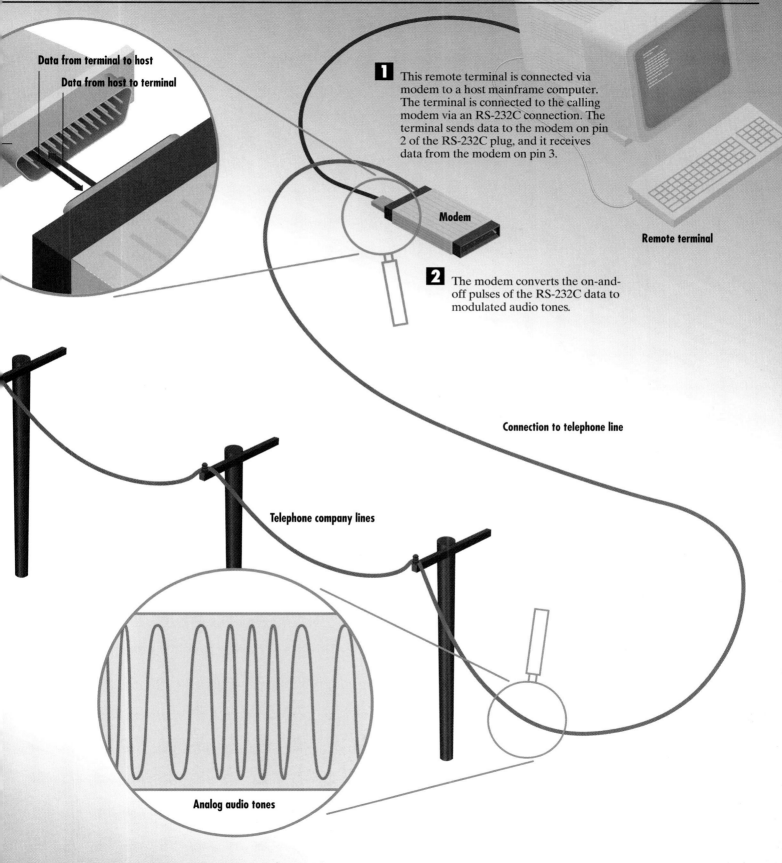

Data from terminal to host

Data from host to terminal

**1** This remote terminal is connected via modem to a host mainframe computer. The terminal is connected to the calling modem via an RS-232C connection. The terminal sends data to the modem on pin 2 of the RS-232C plug, and it receives data from the modem on pin 3.

Modem

Remote terminal

**2** The modem converts the on-and-off pulses of the RS-232C data to modulated audio tones.

Connection to telephone line

Telephone company lines

Analog audio tones

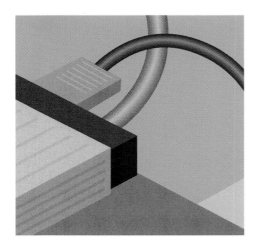

# Mainframes, Time-sharing, and Terminals

**E**ARLY COMPUTER SYSTEMS were very large and very expensive. A typical mainframe computer cost millions of dollars and required several hundred square feet of specially air-conditioned office space. In addition to the hardware, early computers required a full-time staff of programmers and technicians to keep them running. Despite the enormous costs involved, thousands of businesses and universities installed mainframe computer systems in the 1960s and 1970s. Many of those systems are still in use today.

One of the major developments of the 1960s in computing technology was the concept of time-sharing. A time-sharing system allows more than one user—often as many as several hundred—to use the same computer simultaneously. Users could run their own programs, and each user interacted with the computer via a terminal. Most of these early mainframe terminals were mechanical teletypewriter-type units. By the mid-1970s, the video display terminal (VDT) had replaced printing terminals for many applications. Because VDTs often replaced aging teletypewriters, they became known as "glass Teletypes."

In most multiterminal systems, the terminals connect directly to the host computer via a cable. IBM, in typical IBM style, devised its own proprietary system to connect terminals to host computers. However, other manufacturers, including Digital Equipment Corporation, Data General, and Honeywell, use RS-232C connections between the host and the terminals. And for users located away from the main computer site, terminals equipped with modems can be used to access the host computer.

These connections then allowed terminals to move out of the computer room and onto user's desktops. This seemingly simple relocation had a huge effect on the way people used computers. By allowing hundreds of users to share the same computer system, the cost per user spiraled downward. Suddenly, it made economic sense to use computers for such mundane tasks as accounting, classroom scheduling, and even word processing. Before time-sharing, computing was the domain of very large corporations and research institutions. By reducing the cost per user, mainframe computers became affordable for many smaller companies and colleges.

# Host Computer and Terminals

A typical large computer system consists of a host computer system—a mainframe or a minicomputer—and a network of terminals. The terminals, located in the same building as the host, usually connect directly to the host system.

If large branch offices have more than one terminal, a device called a statistical multiplexer can be used to combine the RS-232C signals from the terminals into one multiplexed signal. Another multiplexer at the host computer site reconstructs the individual RS-232C signals from each terminal.

Medium-sized offices requiring full-time access to the host system can be equipped with special leased telephone lines. Although these lines are expensive to install, they are usually cheaper to operate and more reliable than long-distance dial-up lines.

Two banks of modems—one for regular dial-up telephone lines and one for special leased lines—allow off-site access to the host computer.

Small offices needing occasional access to the host computer use a regular voice-grade telephone line and a dial-up modem to access the host system.

# The Personal Computer as a Terminal

**M**OST MAINFRAME AND minicomputer systems, which each may have dozens or even hundreds of terminals attached, allow many users to share the CPU and other computer resources. A typical terminal looks much like a personal computer; it contains a video display, a keyboard, and a serial interface. Unlike a personal computer, a terminal can't do anything unless it is connected to a host computer. When connected, the terminal displays incoming data on the video screen and sends keyboard input to the host computer. Communication with the host computer takes place through the serial interface.

Personal computers first appeared on the computing scene in the late 1970s. In many cases, those early personal computers were purchased by medium and large companies, most of which already had a larger computer system. At first, these computers were used as stand-alone systems; thousands of them were purchased just to run one application such as Lotus 1-2-3, VisiCalc, or WordPerfect. It wasn't unusual to see an office with a personal computer on one corner of a desk and a mainframe terminal at the other. Before long, these same companies learned that by adding a communications program to the personal computer, they could use the computer as a terminal and save all that precious desktop space.

Today, personal computers are routinely used as the access point to the company's mainframe or minicomputer system. Rather than placing both a personal computer and a terminal on everyone's desk, many companies have retired their terminals and replaced them with computers. With the proper communications software, a personal computer can perform all the functions of a terminal. In most cases, a personal computer with communications software actually offers more than the terminal it replaces.

General-purpose communications programs provide terminal emulation, file transfer, and many other features in one package. Although they are designed to operate with modems, most programs provide for direct connections to mainframe and minicomputer systems or to other personal computers.

Since these general-purpose communications programs are oriented toward modems, virtually all provide a convenient way to enter and store phone numbers and communication settings for any number of host computers. Once you've created an entry for a particular host computer in the program's dialing directory, the program can retrieve the entry from the directory and establish a connection automatically.

General-purpose programs usually include a variety of terminal emulations and file transfer protocols. This variety ensures that you'll be able to communicate with almost any dial-up system you may encounter. Some programs include an auto-answer feature, which allows other personal computer users to call your computer and transfer files back and forth.

Most communications programs include a *scripting language* that can automate routine tasks such as connecting to a host computer. Some scripting languages are powerful enough to let you design complete, menu-driven application programs. Many programs include a learn feature, which lets you perform a sequence of tasks while the program watches. Once you've completed the tasks, the program builds a script to replicate your actions. You can then perform the same sequence of tasks at any time by running the script generated by the learn feature. Because they are so flexible, general-purpose programs are the most widely used type of communications software for personal computers.

# The Personal Computer as a Terminal

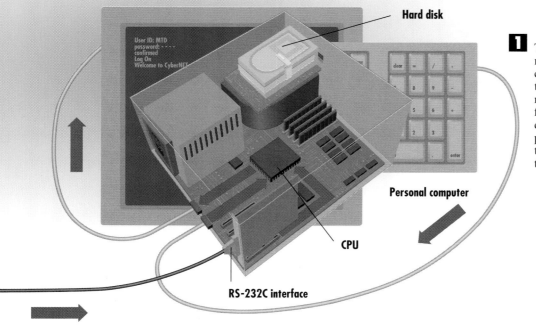

**Hard disk**

**Personal computer**

**CPU**

**RS-232C interface**

**Data from host computer**

**1** The simplest and most common use for personal computer communications software is terminal emulation. In this mode, incoming characters from the host computer are displayed on the personal computer screen, and characters typed on its keyboard are sent to the host computer.

**3** Most personal computer communications programs provide a text upload feature, which allows you to prepare text using a personal computer's word processor or text editor program, and then transmit the text to the host computer. This process doesn't require any special software on the host— as far as the host computer knows, the personal computer is simply a terminal with a very fast, accurate typist.

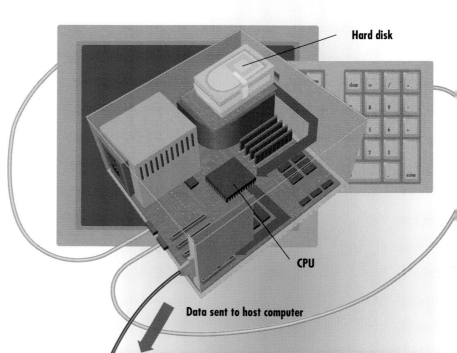

**Hard disk**

**CPU**

**Data sent to host computer**

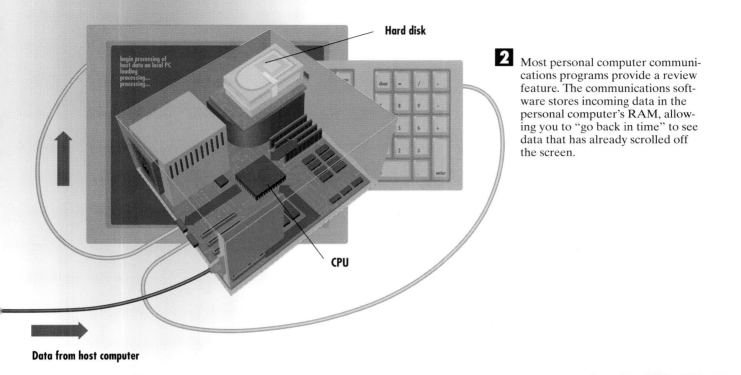

Hard disk

CPU

Data from host computer

**2** Most personal computer communications programs provide a review feature. The communications software stores incoming data in the personal computer's RAM, allowing you to "go back in time" to see data that has already scrolled off the screen.

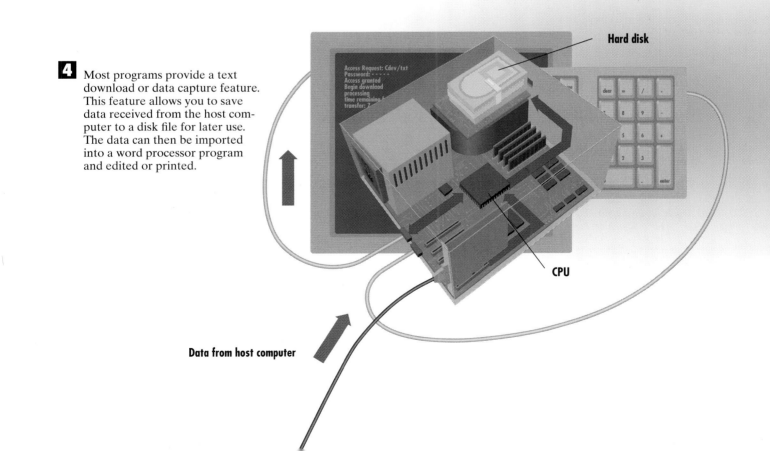

**4** Most programs provide a text download or data capture feature. This feature allows you to save data received from the host computer to a disk file for later use. The data can then be imported into a word processor program and edited or printed.

Hard disk

CPU

Data from host computer

# CHAPTER 12

# Smart Modems

**A**S WE SAW earlier in this book, modems connect the digital universe of computers to the analog world of the telephone network. The earliest modems designed by Bell Labs operated at a maximum speed of 300 bits per second. Almost as soon as the first modems went into service, users began clamoring for faster, more reliable modems. The clamor continues today.

The next step up from the 300-baud Bell 103 modem was another AT&T product, the Bell 212a modem. This modem operated at 1,200 bits per second, or four times the speed of the earlier 103 unit. Although the higher operating speed was a big improvement, the 212a units were very susceptible to noise and signal degradation on the telephone circuit. Even the briefest burst of noise could disrupt communications.

Before the Bell system breakup in 1984, AT&T set virtually all modem standards. Bell Labs' engineers designed new modems, and AT&T's Western Electric division manufactured them. Bell licensed the 103 and 212a technology to other companies, but, with few exceptions, all new modem designs came from AT&T. After the breakup, AT&T was no longer in a position to dictate standards to the rest of the industry.

The Bell breakup coincided with the boom years in personal computer growth. By 1984, the personal computer industry was in the midst of a period of phenomenal growth, which began with the introduction of the IBM Personal Computer in late 1981. The number of personal computers—and modems—in use skyrocketed. The personal computer explosion, coupled with the Bell breakup, presented some unique business opportunities for America's modem manufacturers.

One company in particular, Hayes Microcomputer Products, took the lead in the personal computer modem business. Hayes pioneered the use of microprocessor chips inside the modem itself. The Hayes Smartmodem, first introduced in 1981, used a Zilog Z-8 CPU chip to control the modem circuitry and to provide automatic dialing and answering. Unlike other modems, the Hayes unit could take the phone line off hook, wait for a dial tone, and dial a telephone number all by itself. Hayes Chief Engineer Dale Heatherington once observed that the Hayes Smartmodem had a more powerful CPU than many of the computers it connected.

Like most innovations in the computer industry, the Hayes modem was quickly and mercilessly copied by other modem makers. But Hayes was there first, and it holds one of the key patents relating to intelligent modems.

The next major advance in modem technology was the development of the 2,400-bits-per-second modem in 1985. This time, the technical specification didn't come from Bell Labs, but from the CCITT—an industry standard-setting organization comprising members from hundreds of companies worldwide. The new modem standard was designated V.22bis and is still in wide use today. Other CCITT standards followed, including V.32 (9,600 bits per second), V.32bis (14,400 bits per second), V.42 (error control), and V.42bis (data compression). Virtually all modems in use today conform to one or more of the CCITT standards.

# Inside a Modem

Here's a peek under the hood of a typical 9,600-bps
modem. The modem has four major areas:
power supply, subscriber interface,
CPU, and modem circuitry.

The modem chip performs the complex two-way
conversion between digital signals and analog
sound signals. Without this chip, the modem
circuitry would require thousands of additional
transistors and other electronic components.

Like any computer, the modem's CPU circuitry requires
a steady, regulated source of power. The on-board power-
supply circuitry converts the AC power provided by the
power transformer into regulated DC power.

The central processing unit, or CPU, is the heart of the modem. The CPU controls virtually every other component of the modem and performs the data compression and error detection specified by the CCITT protocols. The CPU's program loads from two ROM chips and uses two 64K RAM chips for temporary storage.

The analog side of the modem begins with the subscriber-line interface, which connects to the telephone network. Overload circuitry protects the modem from lightning and other electrical hazards. Additional circuitry ensures that the modem's output signal conforms to the FCC Part 68 rules.

**CPU**

RS-232C

The RS-232C interface connects the modem to a terminal or host computer. Directed by commands received through the RS-232C port, intelligent modems can store and dial telephone numbers automatically.

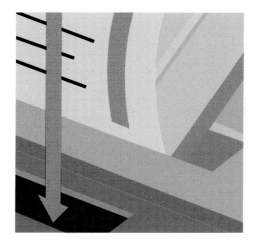

# The Fax Modem

THE FAX HAS taken the world by storm. Barely known ten years ago, modern telephone photo-facsimile machines have permeated the world of business—from the largest corporations to the local pizza parlor.

Some analysts even credit the fax with aiding the spread of democracy. During the periods preceding the reunification of Germany and the breakup of the former Soviet Union, prodemocratic activists used fax machines to distribute news and information.

The fax isn't as new as you might think. Worldwide news services such as Reuters, United Press International, and the Associated Press have used a type of facsimile for years. The U. S. National Oceanic and Atmospheric Administration (NOAA) regularly broadcasts weather information to ships at sea via radio facsimile.

Just as computers communicate by exchanging a series of 1s and 0s, which represent characters in a computer alphabet such as ASCII or EBCDIC, faxes communicate by sending 1s and 0s across the wire. But the 1s and 0s of fax transmissions represent a graphical image of the transmitted page.

A conventional fax is really two machines rolled into one. In any fax transmission, two machines—at opposite ends of the line—play different roles, a sender and a receiver.

The sending machine incorporates an image scanner, a modem, and a microprocessor. The scanner converts the black and white of the transmitted page into 1s and 0s for transmission over the telephone line via the modem. The microprocessor controls the scanner mechanism and compresses the data before transmission.

The receiving machine also uses a modem and microprocessor, and it uses a printing mechanism, as well. The receiving machine reverses the sending process: The modem receives data from the phone and passes the data to the microprocessor. The microprocessor decompresses the data and sends it to the printer, where the 1s and 0s are represented once again as black and white.

If all this sounds like it could be done by a computer, you're right. Enter: the fax modem! Fax modems allow you to use your computer to send and receive faxes. You can save time and paper, you don't need a hard copy, and you don't have to leave your desk to go to the fax machine. As a bonus, PC fax transmissions are sharper and clearer than regular fax transmissions, and computer fax boards don't have any moving parts to cause paper jams.

When receiving incoming fax messages, your fax line rings and the fax modem answers and accepts the incoming fax. The received fax data is then placed on your hard disk. You can use your fax program to view the fax on your screen or to print it. In most cases, computer-printed faxes look as good as or better than conventional fax documents. Plus, you can select the paper—it doesn't have to be the curly, slippery fax paper used by most machines.

Now, the disadvantages of fax modems. If you want to be able to receive faxes any time of the day or night, your computer must be turned on and the fax program must be running—memory resident—at all times. Some communications programs are quite large and reduce the amount of free memory available. Printing is often slow, especially on dot-matrix printers. And, you won't be able to transmit paper documents—you'll need a scanner to first enter these documents into your computer.

# Fax Modem

Although computer fax modems can be used to receive incoming faxes, they excel at transmitting. In this illustration, a fax is being sent from a personal computer to a conventional fax. The fax program on the sending computer must convert the text of the word processed document into a series of 1s and 0s that the receiving fax will understand.

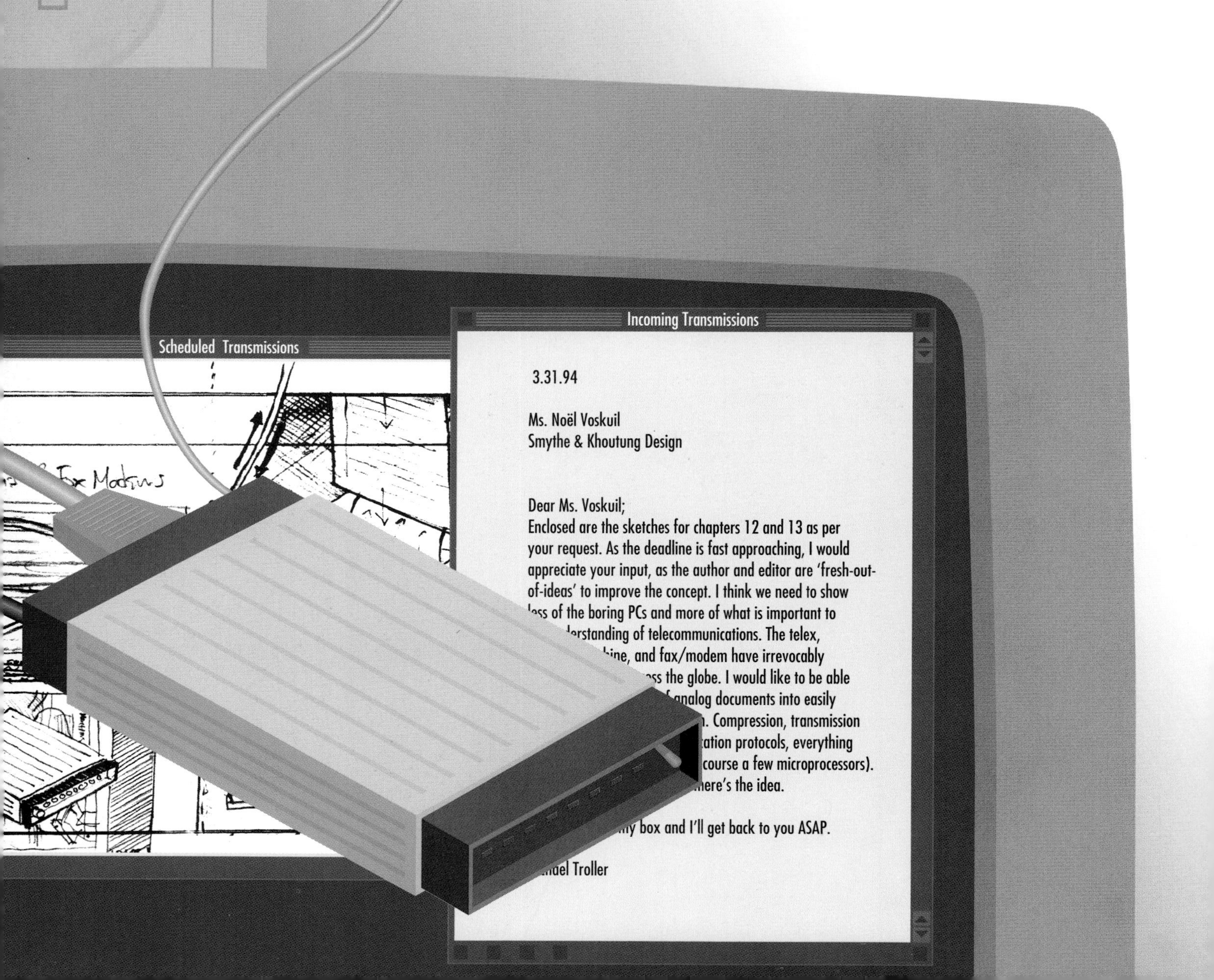

**Scheduled Transmissions**

**Incoming Transmissions**

3.31.94

Ms. Noël Voskuil
Smythe & Khoutung Design

Dear Ms. Voskuil;
Enclosed are the sketches for chapters 12 and 13 as per your request. As the deadline is fast approaching, I would appreciate your input, as the author and editor are 'fresh-out-of-ideas' to improve the concept. I think we need to show less of the boring PCs and more of what is important to understanding of telecommunications. The telex, line, and fax/modem have irrevocably the globe. I would like to be able analog documents into easily Compression, transmission ation protocols, everything course a few microprocessors). here's the idea.

box and I'll get back to you ASAP.

Troller

...approaching, I would
...as the author and editor are 'fresh-out-
...to improve the concept. I think we need to show
less of the boring PCs and more of what is important to
the understanding of telecommunications. The telex,
facsimile machine, and fax/modem have irrevocably
changed business across the globe. I would like to be able
to show the translation of analog documents into easily
manipulated digital information. Compression, transmission
encoding techniques, communication protocols, everything
hinges on the software (and of course a few microprocessors).
A very tall order, I know, but there's the idea.

Call me or beep my box and I'll get back to you ASAP.

Michael Troller

Most fax machines conform to CCITT's Group III standard,
which ensures that all fax machines worldwide can communicate with one another. The CCITT Group III standard
specifies a format of 203 horizontal dots by 98 vertical dots
per inch in standard resolution mode, or about 1,400,000 dots,
or pixels, for a page of text. As far as the receiving fax knows,
the device at the other end of the line is another fax. Since
most faxes and personal computer fax modems conform to
the same Group III standards, compatibility is assured.

# LOCAL AREA NETWORKS (LANS)

CONTENTS

UNTIL NOW, WE'VE focused on how computers communicate—how they transmit and receive data. We looked at how they communicate with each other outside of an office when the distance between them makes it practical to use a modem or a fax instead of a diskette or a piece of paper. In this part of the book, we're going to focus on how computers *interoperate*—how they work together in a network to improve your ability to get things done.

Networks are for sharing. Sharing such things as word processing and spreadsheet files, printers, communication links to distant computers and networks, and electronic mail systems is the function of a network. Every sharing activity, from car pools to bank lines, has its own rules. In networking, we call these rules standards and protocols. *Standards* describe how things should be; typically they set a minimum performance level. *Protocols* are sets of rules and agreements; they describe how elements interact. The key to understanding networking is understanding the standards and protocols that make it possible to interoperate without losing or abusing the shared files and devices.

In this section, we'll talk about standards, protocols, and sharing. First, let's spend a little time learning how many of these standards and protocols came about, then we'll talk more about sharing. Although the standards and protocols for computer communications go back to the work of Morse and Bell at the beginning of this century, the standards and protocols for computer interoperation did not emerge until the early 1980s. Three separate streams fed the computer networking flood: IBM, the U.S. Department of Defense (DOD), and the Xerox Corporation's Palo Alto Research Center. Later, other industry and professional organizations, particularly the Institute of Electrical and Electronic Engineers (the IEEE, pronounced *i-triple-e*) played an important part in developing standards, but the story starts with a computer system called SAGE.

The Semi-Automatic Ground Environment, SAGE, was developed by IBM for the DOD in the 1960s. SAGE, an air-defense system that operated until the mid-1980s, used vacuum-tube computers with memory banks so large that two people could stand inside of them. The computers were installed in pairs in blockhouse buildings, and the filaments from the tubes in a pair of SAGE computers supplied all of the winter heat for large three-story buildings in places such as Great Falls, Montana, and Duluth, Minnesota. The SAGE program involved the efforts of all the best U.S. communications and computer scientists in the 1960s and resulted in a network of interoperating computers that stretched across the United States. The program was the equivalent of the Golden Spike that linked the railroads in 1869. SAGE proved the practicality of interoperating computer systems and stimulated development efforts, particularly by IBM and the federal government.

In the 1970s, the DOD—faced with an inventory of different computers that could not interoperate—pioneered the development of network software protocols that work on more than one make and model of computer. The major set of protocols established by the DOD is the Transmission Control Protocol /Internet Protocol (TCP/IP). As the name implies, these protocols are agreements on how transmission takes place across networks. Companies, particularly those that want the federal government's business, write software that conforms to those protocols.

At about the same time in the 1970s, IBM began making public the standards and protocols it used for its proprietary computer systems. The standards included detailed descriptions of cabling, and the protocols were designed to ensure accurate communications under heavy loads. This work led others to emulate IBM's techniques and raised the quality of network development in the entire industry. It also led to an uprising by other computer companies that objected to IBM's total control of the most widely used standards and protocols. Eventually, this uprising led to the flexibility and interoperability we enjoy today.

Computer interoperation involves moving a lot of data, but it's difficult to move a lot of anything, including data, over a long distance. So computer interoperation usually begins with computers in the same office or the same building connected to a local network. The term *local area network,* or *LAN* (rhymes with *pan*), describes a group of computers typically connected by no more than 1,000 feet of cable, which interoperate and allow people to share resources.

In the 1970s, IBM and Digital Equipment Corporation developed ways for a few large computers to interoperate over local networks, but the most important work on LANs for a large number of computers was done at the Xerox Corporation's Palo Alto Research Center (PARC) in the late 1970s and early 1980s. At PARC, an important set of standards and protocols called Ethernet was conceived and developed to the point of becoming a commercial product. At about the same time, people working independently at Datapoint Corporation developed a standard called ARCnet, but Datapoint kept ARCnet as a proprietary set of specifications so it didn't have the commercial success of Ethernet. Later, IBM developed the third major networking technology we use today, Token-Ring.

The early local area network architectures, such as Ethernet and ARCnet, combined inflexible hardware specifications with strict protocol descriptions. Specific types of copper cable, specific cable connectors, one physical configuration, and certain software functions were bundled together in each LAN definition. But because of the government and industry push for flexibility, the single simple set of specifications and descriptions for each type of network has expanded to include different types of cables, configurations, and protocols. Today, you can mix and match hardware and software to create a customized network and still stay within a network system specification supported by products from many different companies.

During the mid-1980s, a group of manufacturers started a movement toward what are called open protocols—protocols that do not favor a single manufacturer. Many manufacturers worked at developing software written to open protocol standards, but in the early 1990s, the movement lost momentum. The emphasis changed from developing a single set of new, openly published protocols to making practical use of the tried-and-true protocols of different manufacturers. As programmers and developers learned more about protocols and developed more programs and tools, they found ways to make different computers and networks interoperate without moving to a single rigid, but open standard. Today, it is easy to mix Macintosh and IBM-style personal computers on the same network and to interoperate among computers attached to different types of networks.

At the same time, new families of programs make it easier to share files and resources, such as printers and modems. In the 1980s, developers created the word processing, spreadsheet, and database programs that people use to create data files. In the 1990s, developers introduced new categories of software, referred to as workgroup productivity programs and workflow software, which make it easy to search for, organize, and link data from documents, spreadsheets, and databases so that it can be shared. Sharing now means more than just waiting in a queue to use a file or a printer. We have gone beyond the old computer model of data handling—which was like checking out one book at a time from the library to do research—and moved to new workgroup productivity programs that are the equivalent of having the librarian find the desired paragraph or reference, read it aloud to you, make a copy, and file it with other copies on the same subject. The availability of processed information transmitted over networks makes it possible for people to work faster and to work with fewer resources. This allows more people to work independently, to work at home, and to keep flexible hours.

Over a short few decades, the computer network industry has made more progress across a broad front than even the personal computer industry. The network evolution has swept along with it telephone technology, computer hardware design, software design, and even workgroup sociology. Today, both computers and buildings come with their networking components in place. If you have new equipment and a new building, you can add the software of your choice, plug a cable into a wall jack, and interoperate across a LAN. Wireless networks, both high-speed local networks and slower world-wide networks, link portable computers with a central business location. Modern networks mix handwritten and typed words, voice and sound, and graphics and video conferencing on the same cable. Networks make it possible for organizations to abandon the top-down management structure—that is, where a lot of information was held at the top—and move on to a flatter, more responsive structure where information is shared and widely available. Networks change the way we work, so now let's find out how they work!

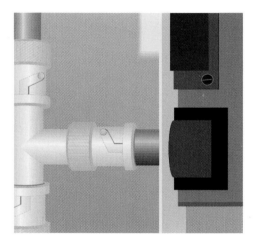

# A Network Model

LET'S BEGIN OUR investigation of networks by looking at their components to see how they relate to one another and connect. Then, in subsequent chapters we'll look inside each network component to see how it works. Here are the major components of a network:

**Network Operating System**   The network operating system, or NOS (rhymes with *boss*) consists of a family of programs that run in the networked computers. Some programs provide the ability to share files, printers, and other devices across the network. Computers that share their resources are called *servers*. Other programs that give the ability to use those shared resources are called *clients*. It is common to have client and server software running in the same computer, so you can use the resources on other computers while your coworkers make use of your disk space, printers, or communications devices.

**Networked Peripherals**   In 1991, a new category of products called networked peripherals became generally available; these include printers and modems with their own network connections. Network peripherals have internal specialized processors to run networking server software, so they don't have to be directly attached to a computer. Application programs running on client Macintosh computers and PCs can use a networked printer or modem as if it were locally attached.

**Network Interface Card (LAN Adapter)**   The low-powered digital signals inside a computer aren't powerful enough to travel long distances, so a device called a network interface card changes the signals inside a computer into more powerful signals that can cross a network cable. After the network interface card takes the data from the computer, it has the important jobs of packaging the data for transmission and acting as a gatekeeper to control access to the shared network cable.

**Network Cabling**   The computers in modern networks can send messages in the form of electrical pulses over copper cable of different kinds, over fiber optic cable using pulses of light, or through the air using radio or light waves. In fact, you can combine all these techniques in one network to meet specific needs or to take advantage of what is already installed. Modern network cabling installations use a central wiring hub.

# A Network Model

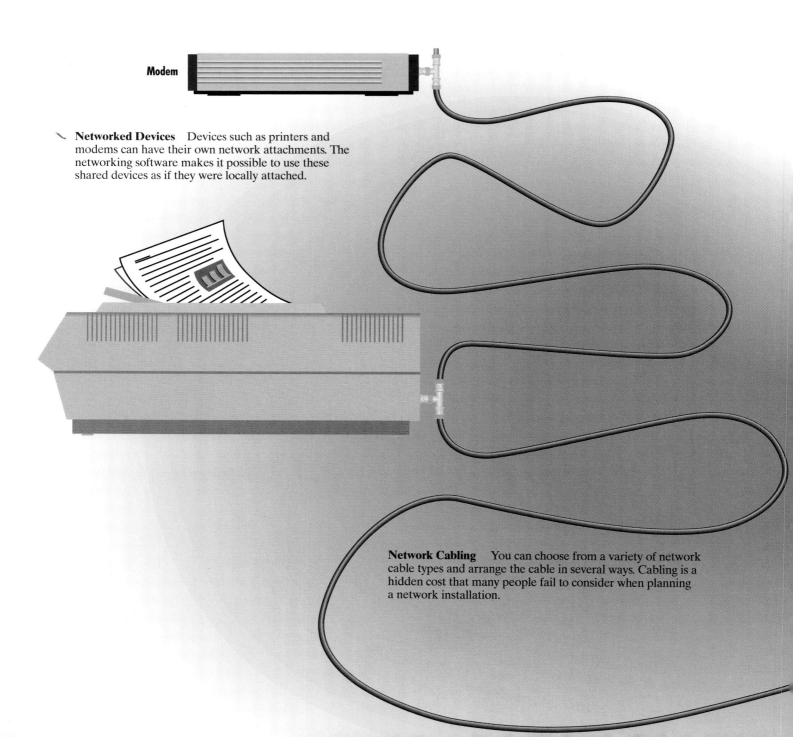

Modem

**Networked Devices** Devices such as printers and modems can have their own network attachments. The networking software makes it possible to use these shared devices as if they were locally attached.

**Network Cabling** You can choose from a variety of network cable types and arrange the cable in several ways. Cabling is a hidden cost that many people fail to consider when planning a network installation.

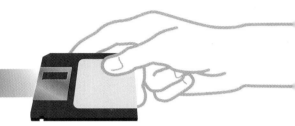

*   **Networking Software**    Networking software can be a
    special program you add, such as Novell's NetWare or
    Artisoft's LANtastic, or it can be part of an operating
    system, such as Microsoft's Windows for Workgroups.
    Macintosh computers have built-in networking software
    that can interoperate with these products.

**Network Interface Card**    Network interface cards link the computer to
the network cable system. The card controls the flow of data between
the computer's internal data bus and the serial stream of data on the
network cable. Some computers come with their own network interface
cards on the motherboard, and some interface adapters attach to a computer's parallel port, but the cards are usually added to the computer's
expansion bus.

# Network Operating Systems

**N**ETWORK OPERATING SYSTEMS, products offered by companies such as Artisoft, Microsoft, and Novell, are actually a combination of programs that give some computers and peripherals the ability to accept requests for service across the network and give other computers the ability to correctly use those services. Servers are computers that share their hard-disk drives, attached peripherals such as printers and CD-ROM drives, and communications circuits. Servers inspect requests for proper authorization, check for conflicts, and then provide the requested service.

*File servers* store files created by application programs. In some configurations, the file servers might also hold the application programs themselves. A file server is a computer that has a hard-disk drive large enough to share. File servers provide economy, because many people can store their data on a single hard-disk drive, and they also offer the ability to simultaneously access the same file. People who update databases, customer-service representatives taking phone orders, for example, need to use the same inventory and financial data files at the same time. File-server software allows shared access to specific segments of the data files under controlled conditions.

*Print servers* accept print jobs sent by anyone across the network. Since even the fastest print jobs typically still take 5 to 10 seconds per page, *spooling* the print jobs (saving them in a disk file until the printer is ready to accept them) is a critical function of the print-server software. The print-server software also reports the status of jobs waiting for printing and recognizes the priorities assigned to specific users. Computers can run both the file-server and print-server software, or print-server software can run in specialized processors inside networked printers or in small self-contained print-server devices. Practically any number of printers can be shared on a single network in a variety of ways.

*Client software* works with the internal operating system of a computer so it can route requests from application programs and from the keyboard out to file servers and print servers on the network. The principal element of the client software is called a *redirector*. As its name implies, the redirector captures service requests it has been programmed to recognize and routes them out of the PC and across the network for service. Typically, redirector software has to be added to an IBM-style PC, but is part of the Macintosh operating system and part of Microsoft's Windows for Workgroups. In some network operating systems, it is common to run the client software with file- or print-server software in the same computer.

Network communications software packages requests from the client computers and sends the requests across the network. This software conforms to specific protocols for addressing, ensuring delivery, and ensuring accuracy. Typical suites of network communications protocols include Apple's Apple File Protocol (AFP), Artisoft's Network Basic Input Output System (NetBIOS, pronounced *NET-bi-ous*), Microsoft's NetBIOS Extended User Interface (NETBEUI, pronounced *NET-boo-ee*), and Novell's Sequential Packet Exchange and Internetwork Packet Exchange (SPX and IPX).

You'll often hear networking people discuss the problem of having the proper *drivers*. The driver software works between the network interface card and the network communications software. At one time, you had to generate a special configuration of the network operating system for every make and model of LAN adapter on the market. Today, if an adapter manufacturer supplies drivers conforming to Microsoft's Network Driver Interface Standard (NDIS, pronounced *N-diss*) or Novell's Open Data-Link Interface (ODI), you can use that adapter with a variety of network operating systems. Companies now deliver standardized drivers, so you are free to buy interface cards from different vendors.

# A Network Operating System

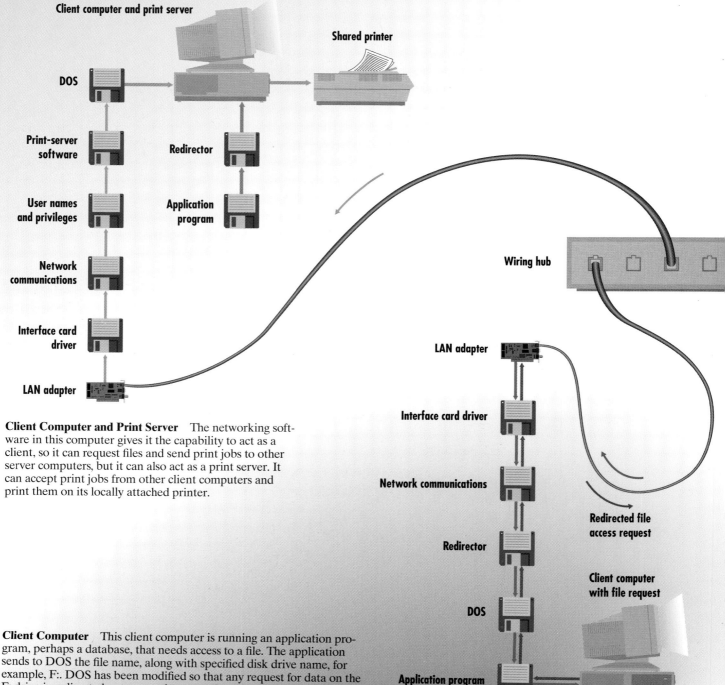

Client computer and print server

Shared printer

DOS

Print-server
software

Redirector

User names
and privileges

Application
program

Network
communications

Interface card
driver

LAN adapter

Wiring hub

LAN adapter

Interface card driver

Network communications

Redirected file
access request

Redirector

Client computer
with file request

DOS

Application program

**Client Computer and Print Server**   The networking software in this computer gives it the capability to act as a
client, so it can request files and send print jobs to other
server computers, but it can also act as a print server. It
can accept print jobs from other client computers and
print them on its locally attached printer.

**Client Computer**   This client computer is running an application program, perhaps a database, that needs access to a file. The application
sends to DOS the file name, along with specified disk drive name, for
example, F:. DOS has been modified so that any request for data on the
F: drive is redirected out across the network to the file server.

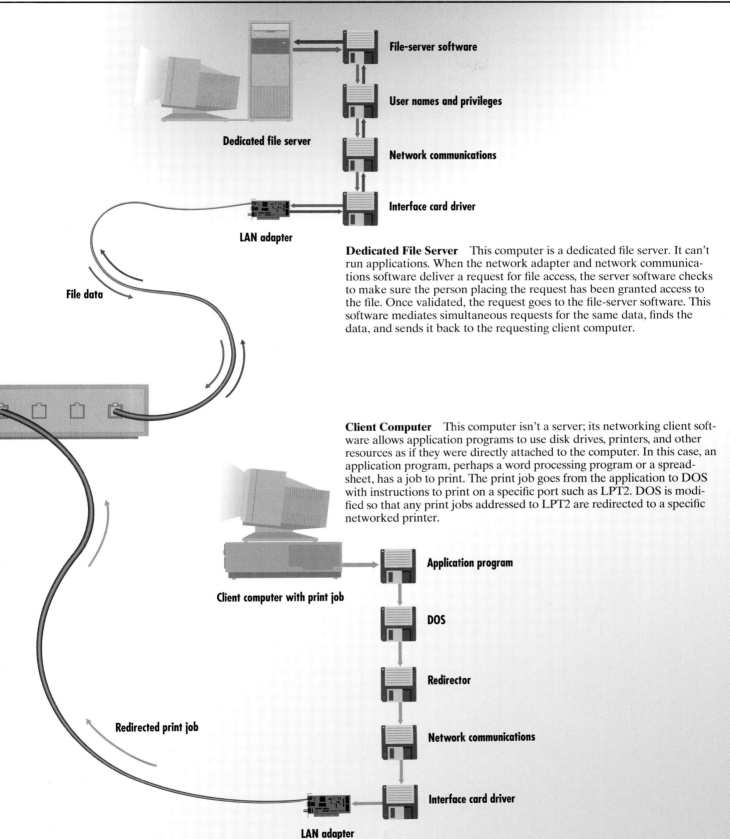

**File-server software**

**User names and privileges**

**Network communications**

**Interface card driver**

**Dedicated file server**

**LAN adapter**

**File data**

**Dedicated File Server** This computer is a dedicated file server. It can't run applications. When the network adapter and network communications software deliver a request for file access, the server software checks to make sure the person placing the request has been granted access to the file. Once validated, the request goes to the file-server software. This software mediates simultaneous requests for the same data, finds the data, and sends it back to the requesting client computer.

**Client Computer** This computer isn't a server; its networking client software allows application programs to use disk drives, printers, and other resources as if they were directly attached to the computer. In this case, an application program, perhaps a word processing program or a spreadsheet, has a job to print. The print job goes from the application to DOS with instructions to print on a specific port such as LPT2. DOS is modified so that any print jobs addressed to LPT2 are redirected to a specific networked printer.

**Application program**

**DOS**

**Redirector**

**Network communications**

**Interface card driver**

**Client computer with print job**

**Redirected print job**

**LAN adapter**

# A Network Operating System

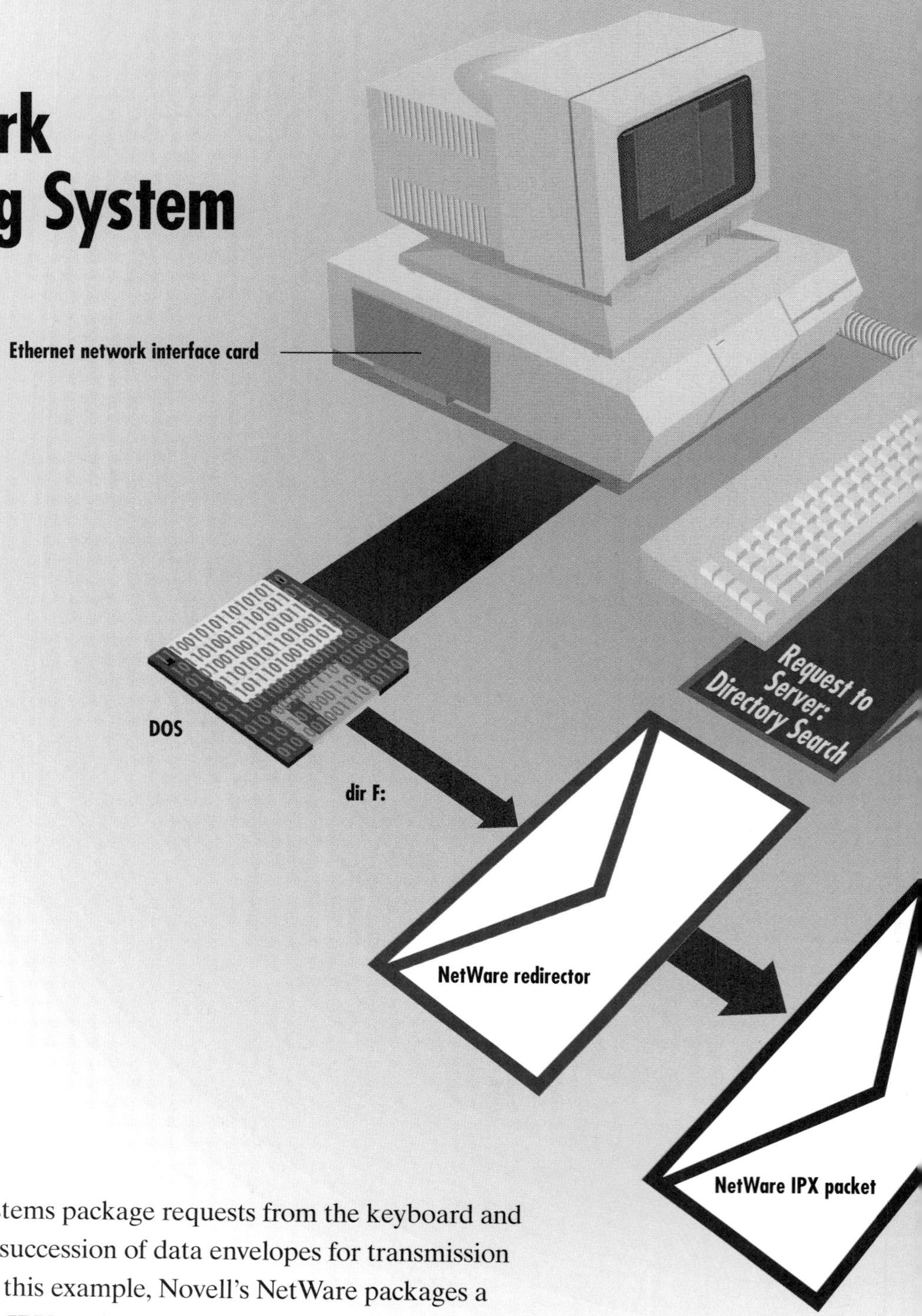

Ethernet network interface card

DOS

dir F:

Request to Server: Directory Search

NetWare redirector

NetWare IPX packet

Network operating systems package requests from the keyboard and from applications in a succession of data envelopes for transmission across the network. In this example, Novell's NetWare packages a directory request in an IPX packet, and the LAN adapter packages the IPX request into an Ethernet frame. Each data envelope contains its own addressing and error-control information.

Keyboard entry: dir F:

Data Field
Source Socket
Source Host
Source Network
Destination Source
Destination Host
Destination Network
Packet Type
Length
Error Control

Error Control
Data Field
Packet Length
Ethernet Source Address
Ethernet Destination Address
Synchronization Preamble

Ethernet frame

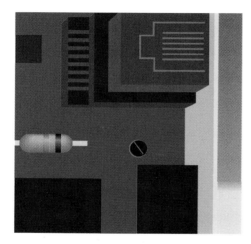

# The Network Interface Card

THE NETWORK INTERFACE card, or LAN adapter, functions as an interface between the computer and the network cabling, so it must serve two masters. Inside the computer, it moves data to and from the random access memory (RAM). Outside the computer, it controls the flow of data in and out of the network cable system. An interface card has a specialized port that matches the electrical signaling standards used on the cable and the specific type of cable connector. In between the computer and the cable, the interface card must buffer the data, because the computer is typically much faster than the network. The interface card also must change the form of the data from a wide parallel stream coming in 8 bits at a time to a narrow stream moving 1 bit at a time in and out of the network port.

These jobs require some on-board processing power, and LAN adapters have processors specially designed for the task. A wide variety of companies, including Artisoft, IBM, Intel, National Semiconductor, and Texas Instruments, sell special-purpose processors and supporting chips for network adapters. These processors are augmented by 8 to 64K of RAM and by specialized *transceivers* that handle the electrical interface to the cable. Some adapters have a socket for a special read-only memory chip called a *boot ROM,* which allows a PC to start DOS from a file on a server—eliminating the need for an internal hard disk-drive.

You must select a network interface card that matches your computer's data bus and the network cable. This seems like a simple concept, but there are many combinations possible. A Macintosh and a high-end IBM PS/2 have very different data bus connections. Even among otherwise similar PCs, the task of choosing between the industry standard architecture (ISA) bus of the old IBM PC AT and the newer Extended Industry Standard Architecture (EISA) bus, pioneered by Compaq and other companies, is confusing. Our testing shows that EISA adapters prove their worth in computers acting as servers, but that ISA adapters are fine for most desktop PC systems. If you use adapters for the EISA bus or the IBM PS/2 Microchannel Architecture (MCA), you can also choose products using *bus-mastering,* a more efficient method of moving data to and from the computer's memory. Bus-mastering lightens the load on the computer's processor by moving data to and from the computer's RAM without interrupting the processor, but this technique requires more processing power on the adapter board so these boards cost more. Choose bus-mastering adapters for very busy servers.

On the network cable side, the LAN adapter performs three important functions: It generates the electrical signals that travel over the network cable; it follows specific rules controlling access to the cable; and it makes the physical connection to the cable. Adapters for Ethernet and Token-Ring both use the same basic system of electrical signaling over the cable. Surprisingly, the signals on these high-speed computer cables aren't very different from the early Morse code or Baudot teletype code. A technique called Manchester encoding provides a way to transmit 0s and 1s using direct current voltage pulses that range from –15 to +15 volts. The LAN adapters translate each change in the voltage level as a character in the ASCII data alphabet.

The technique the adapters use to control access to the cable and the type of cable connectors are attributes of the network architecture, such as Ethernet or Token-Ring, that you choose. We'll describe network architectures more thoroughly in the next chapter, but you should know that you will need adapters with the right connectors and the right protocols for access into the network cable.

# Network Interface Card

A network interface card, or LAN adapter, uses a specialized processor and routines stored in memory to move data to and from the computer's memory over the parallel data bus and to transmit and receive data on the serial network cable. It rearranges and buffers the data while handling the interface to the computer and the interface to the cable.

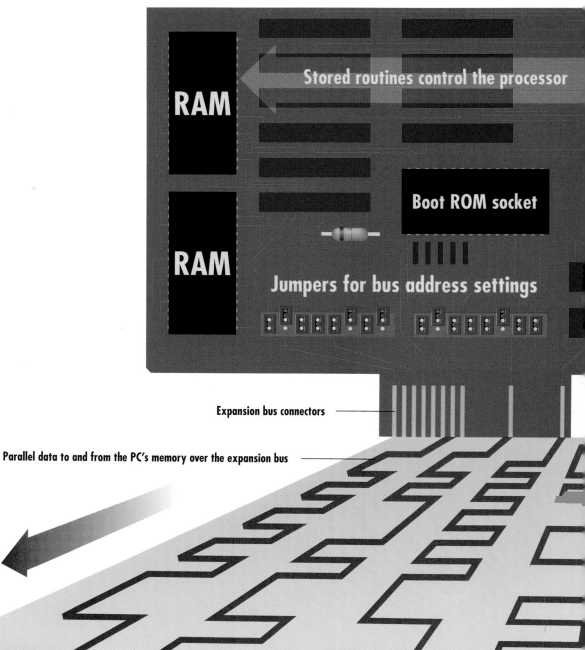

Stored routines control the processor

RAM

Boot ROM socket

RAM

Jumpers for bus address settings

Expansion bus connectors

Parallel data to and from the PC's memory over the expansion bus

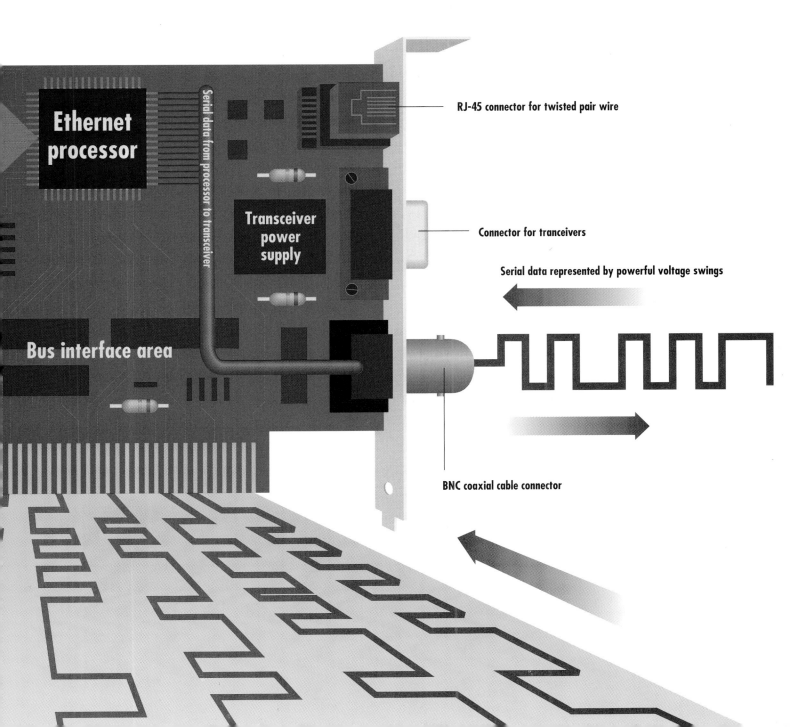

Ethernet processor

Serial data from processor to transceiver

Transceiver power supply

Bus interface area

RJ-45 connector for twisted pair wire

Connector for tranceivers

Serial data represented by powerful voltage swings

BNC coaxial cable connector

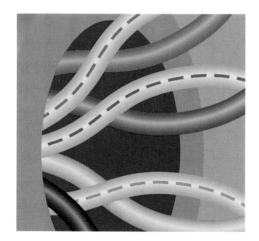

CHAPTER 17

# Network Cabling

**T**HE NETWORK INTERFACE cards and network operating system can't work without reliable and high-quality connections between the network nodes. When you select your network cabling, you face an array of standards and options. ARCnet, Ethernet, and Token-Ring are the three most commonly accepted sets of standards for controlling network signaling, cable access, and cable configurations. However, a new set of standards for cabling has emerged that overrides the cable standards established previously within each networking scheme. In the following pages, we'll illustrate the classic wiring configurations associated with each scheme as well as a new structured wiring system; we'll also examine LAN cable standards and wireless networking.

The network cable, or *media* as it's called in LAN-speak, is a single thread of copper or glass that links all the nodes on the network, but it can only carry the signals from one network interface card at a time. Thus each LAN architecture needs a media-access control (MAC) scheme so network interface cards can take turns transmitting into the cable.

In an Ethernet network, the interface cards share the common cable by listening before they transmit and transmitting only during a break in the traffic when the channel is quiet, a technique called *carrier-sense multiple access with collision detection* (CSMA/CD). With collision detection, if two stations begin to transmit at the same time, they detect the collision, stop, and retry after a sufficient time interval.

Token-Ring network interface cards use a much more complex media-access control scheme called *token-passing*. Ethernet cards contend for access to the cable; Token-Ring cards must have permission to transmit into a cable system that forms a complete electrical loop or ring. Under this technique, the active cards negotiate, using their built-in serial numbers, to determine a master interface card. The master initiates a special message called a free token. When an interface card with data to send receives a free token, it changes the free token into a message and sends it to the next station up the ring for relay. After the addressed interface card receives the message and the message returns to the originating interface card, that card initiates a new free token and the process begins again.

ARCnet network interface cards use a somewhat similar media-access control scheme. A master card, designated by the lowest number set into the cards through switches, maintains a table of all active cards and polls each one in turn, giving permission to transmit.

Network interface cards, also called LAN adapters, provide a wide variety of physical connections for the network cables. The trappings on the cables range from shiny metal Ethernet T-connectors to the simple plastic modular plugs used with unshielded twisted pair wire (UTP). Some Ethernet cards have connectors for coaxial cable, and others provide a 15-pin socket for more complex external transceivers for fiber optic and other types of cables. Token-Ring cards have a 9-pin connector for shielded twisted pair wire (STP). However, unshielded twisted pair wire is becoming increasingly popular for both Token-Ring and Ethernet cards. These cards have a simple plastic rectangular jack similar to those found on modern telephones.

Modern network cable installations conform to specifications for structured wiring systems issued by the Electronic Industries Association and Underwriter's Laboratories. This architecture uses wire without an external shield of copper braid, but each pair of wires is twisted together at about six turns per inch. The twisting cancels electric currents—absorbed from power cables and other outside sources—that can mask the network signals. Structured wiring systems improve reliability by using dedicated spans of wire from each node to a central wiring hub. The hub automatically disconnects malfunctioning interface cards and defective wire spans so they don't degrade the rest of the network.

Some specialized network interface cards do not use copper cables. They can read pulses of laser light sent over fiber optic cables, pulses of invisible infrared light sent through the air, and signals imposed on radio waves. Modern installations often use copper cables for most connections and intermix fiber optic or wireless alternatives to reach special nodes.

LAN cables come in many physical configurations. Important selection considerations include resistance to *crosstalk*—electric currents between pairs of wires in the same cable—resistance to outside electrical fields caused by power lines, motors, relays, radio transmitters, and other devices; and ease of installation. If a cable resists internal and external electrical noise, network designers can use longer cables and faster signaling between nodes. Because fiber optic cables signal with pulses of light, they have total immunity from electrical noise. Fiber optic cables carry signals faster and farther than any other type of cable. Cables with outside shields of copper braid or foil, such as coaxial and shielded twisted pair, offer good resistance to electrical noise. But because they are thicker, they are difficult to pull through wiring conduits and walls. The thin unshielded twisted pair wire is easier to install, but it offers less resistance to electrical noise. Thin fiber optic cable doesn't fill conduits, but installers need special training and equipment to attach connectors, so the costs for fiber optic cable are high. As a final consideration, remember that the outer jackets of cables used inside air plenums and between floors must have special fire-resistant jackets to resist the spread of fire and the creation of toxic gas when exposed to flame.

Your network's operating system and even its network interface cards can be changed in a few hours or days. But changing the cabling requires weeks of work. Cable selection and installation are important steps in designing a network that will serve you economically and reliably for years. Study the options and carefully specify your needs.

# Unshielded Twisted Pair (UTP) Wire

This cable typically combines four pairs of wires inside the same outer jacket. Each pair is twisted with a different number of twists per inch. The twisting cancels out electrical noise from adjacent pairs and from other devices in the building such as motors, relays, and transformers. Although unshielded twisted pair externally resembles common telephone wire, telephone wire lacks the twisting and other electrical characteristics needed to carry data.

SPEED & THROUGHPUT

FAST ENOUGH

AVERAGED COST PER NODE

LEAST EXPENSIVE

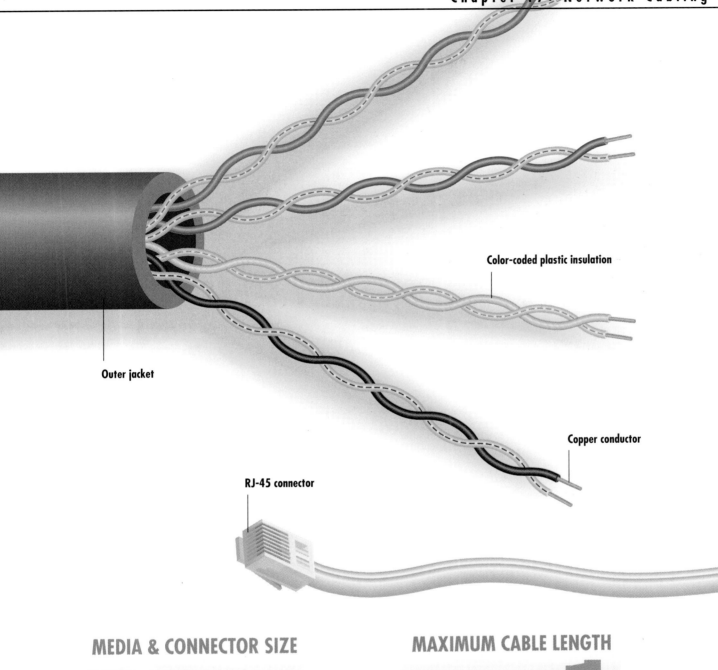

Color-coded plastic insulation

Copper conductor

Outer jacket

RJ-45 connector

## MEDIA & CONNECTOR SIZE

SMALL

## MAXIMUM CABLE LENGTH

SHORT

# Coaxial Cable

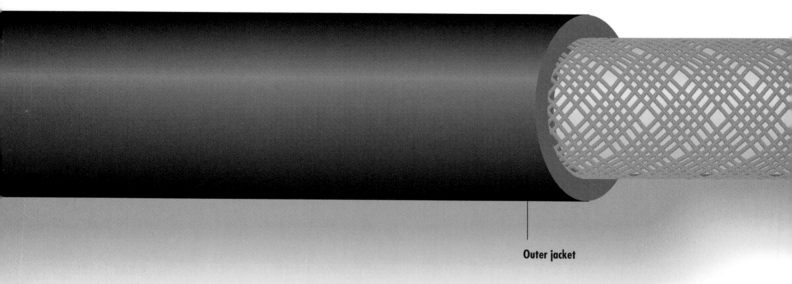

Outer jacket

This cable gets its name from the two conductors that share the same center axis; they are coaxial. Coaxial cable relies on woven copper braid to shield the center conductor from outside electric currents. The Ethernet and ARCnet specifications both include coaxial cable, but they each call for a different type of cable.

SPEED & THROUGHPUT

VERY FAST

AVERAGED COST PER NODE

INEXPENSIVE

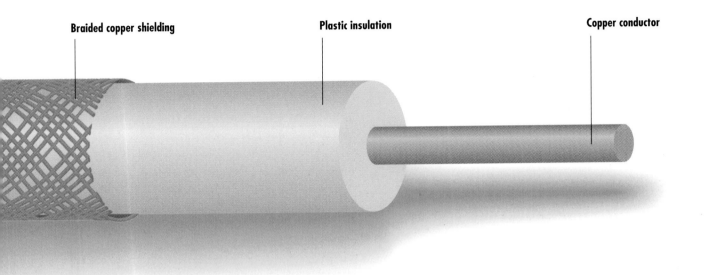

Braided copper shielding

Plastic insulation

Copper conductor

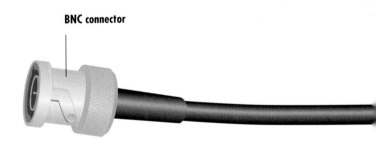

BNC connector

MEDIA & CONNECTOR SIZE

MEDIUM

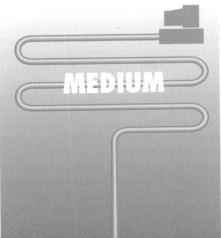

MAXIMUM CABLE LENGTH

MEDIUM

# Shielded Twisted Pair Wire (STP)

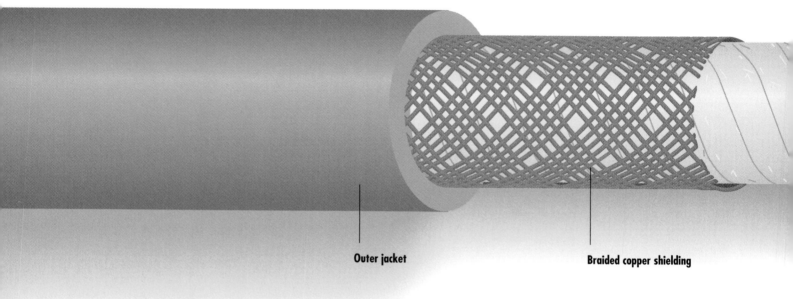

Outer jacket

Braided copper shielding

This cable, called for only in the Token-Ring LAN specifications, uses a woven copper braid, a foil wrap between and around the wire pairs, and internal twisting of the pairs to provide a high degree of protection from outside electric currents. However, the combination creates a thick cable that rapidly fills the space in building wiring ducts.

SPEED & THROUGHPUT

VERY FAST

AVERAGED COST PER NODE

EXPENSIVE

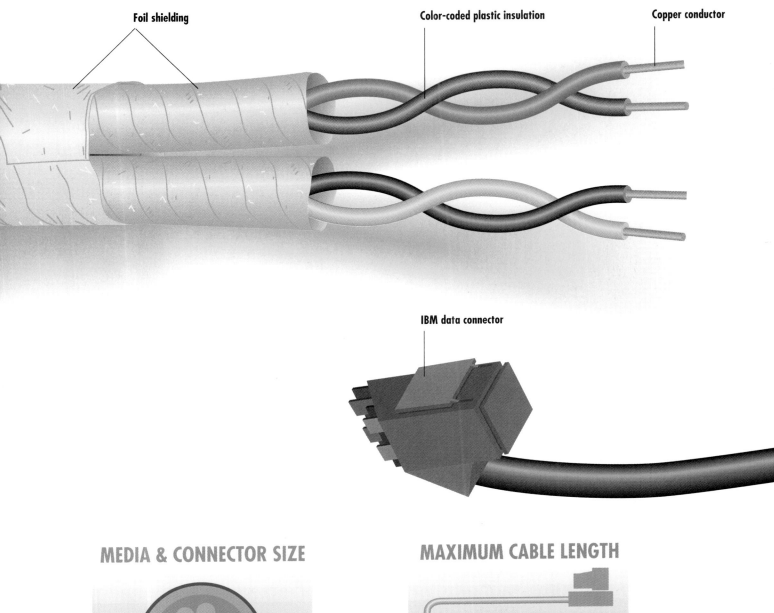

Foil shielding

Color-coded plastic insulation

Copper conductor

IBM data connector

## MEDIA & CONNECTOR SIZE

LARGE

## MAXIMUM CABLE LENGTH

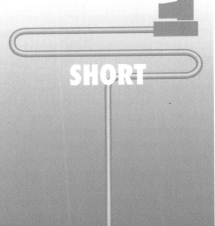

SHORT

# Fiber Optic Cable

Outer jacket

Because the signals it carries are pulses of light conducted over threads of glass, fiber optic cables aren't bothered by outside electric currents. Each glass strand only passes signals in one direction, so a cable has two strands in separate jackets. Each jacket has a group of Kevlar fibers for strength, and a reinforcing layer of plastic surrounds the glass strand. Special connectors make an optically pure connection to the glass fiber and provide a window for laser transmitters and optical receivers. Because they are free of interference and the light pulses travel for miles without losing appreciable strength, fiber optic cables can carry data at high signaling speeds over long distances.

**SPEED & THROUGHPUT**

FASTEST POSSIBLE

**AVERAGED COST PER NODE**

MOST EXPENSIVE

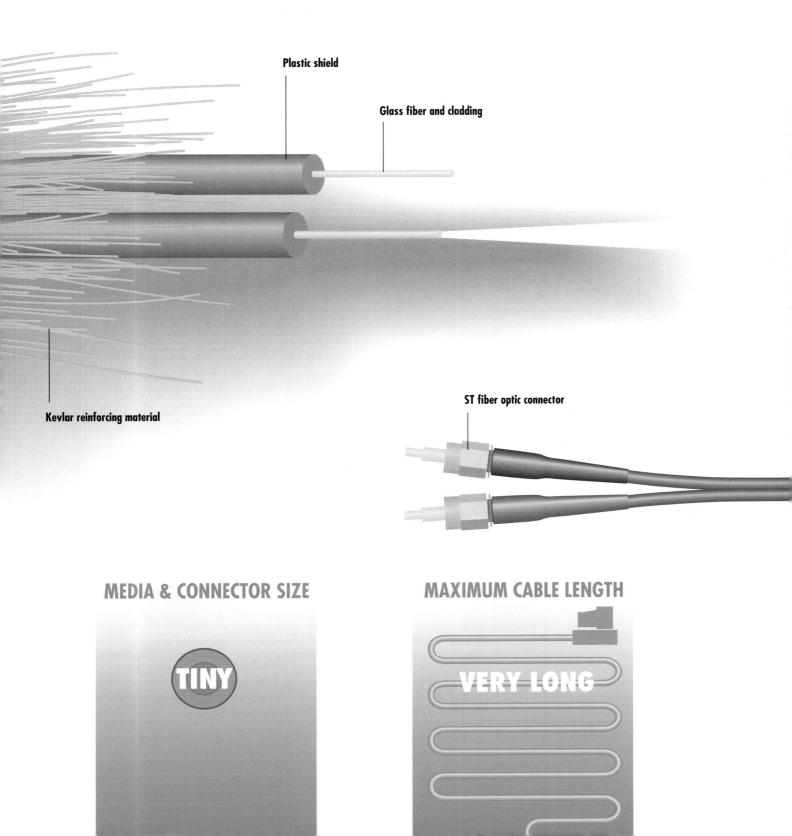

Plastic shield

Glass fiber and cladding

Kevlar reinforcing material

ST fiber optic connector

MEDIA & CONNECTOR SIZE

TINY

MAXIMUM CABLE LENGTH

VERY LONG

# Ethernet Networking

**Terminator**

**T-connector with terminator**

On the left, you see computers connected by a cable that runs from interface card to interface card. This configuration saves cable and is easy to install in small groups, but if the cable breaks at any point, it disrupts network operation of all the computers on that cable.

**T-connector**

**BNC connector**

The linear bus, or thin Ethernet, cable configuration uses a T-shaped coaxial connector at each interface card. Each end of the coaxial cable has a terminator, which absorbs signals when they reach the ends of the cable and prevents their reflection.

**T-connector**

**Thin Ethernet coaxial cable**

**T-connector**

Although network interface cards usually reside in computer expansion slots, you can connect to computers that don't have slots, such as laptops, using an external network interface card. You can choose from adapters with coaxial or unshielded twisted pair wire connectors.

**External network interface card**

**Wiring hub**

A wiring hub provides a central point for the cables attached to each network interface card. You can select hubs with connectors for coaxial, fiber optic, and twisted pair wire. In this example, the hub connects to the thin Ethernet linear bus of coaxial cable and has a strip of connectors for unshielded twisted pair wire.

**Unshielded twisted pair wire used in 10BaseT configurations**

**RJ-45 connector**

The Ethernet configuration using unshielded twisted pair wire is known as 10BaseT because it uses 10 megabit per second (Mbps) signaling speed, direct current, or baseband, signaling, and twisted pair wire. This configuration includes a central wiring hub with special circuitry to isolate malfunctioning segments of the network. Unshielded twisted pair wire uses a small plastic connector called an RJ-45 connector at each end of the wire.

# Token-Ring Network

This Token-Ring network has one network with two physically separate wiring hubs. The hubs, connected by fiber optic cable, can be thousands of feet apart. The computers and other networked devices, connected by either shielded or unshielded twisted pair wires, must be within approximately 100 feet of the wiring hub. The packages of data, called *frames,* move from node to node in a circle, but the wiring is in a star configuration. The actual ring in a Token-Ring network exists within the wiring hubs.

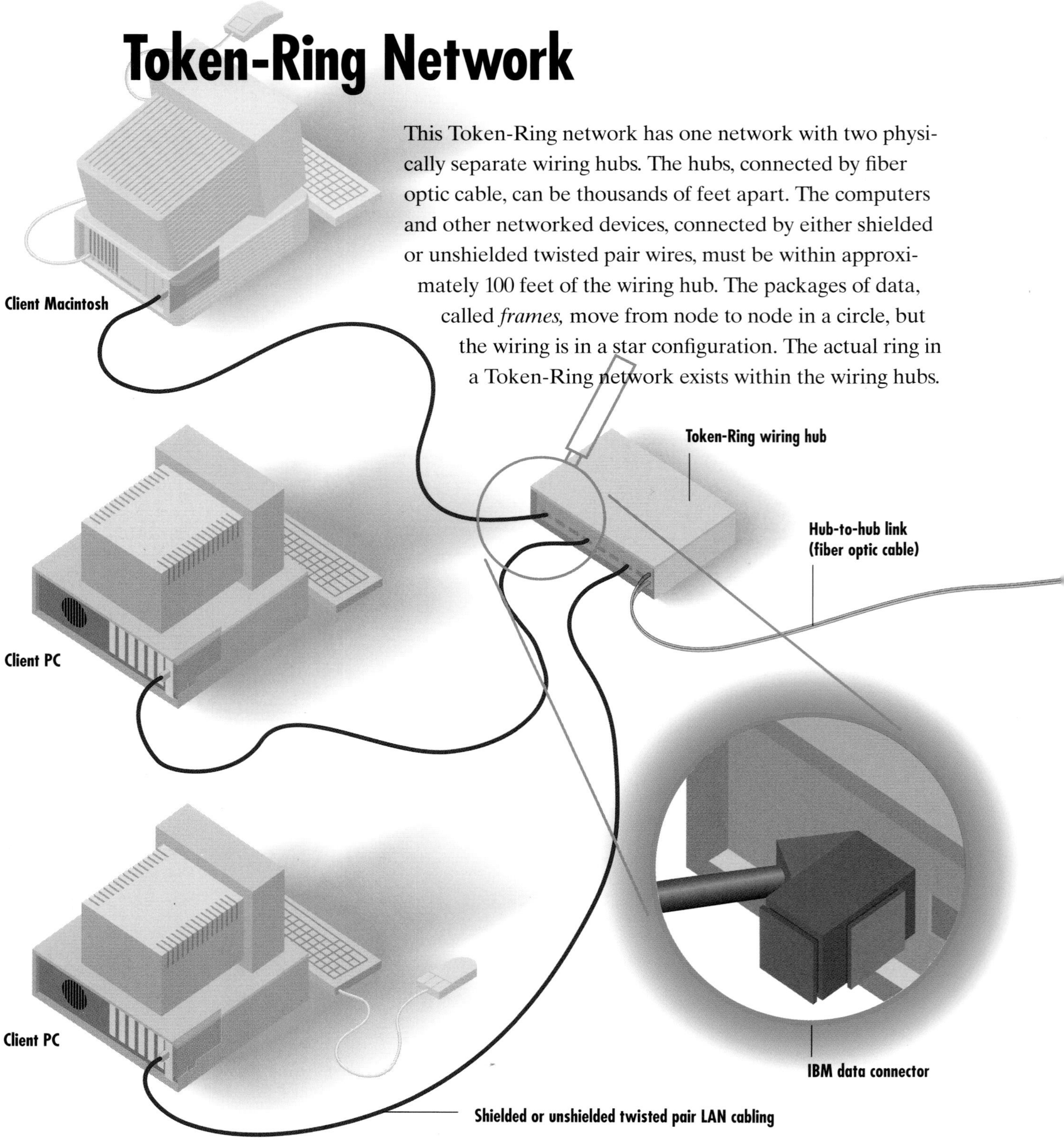

**Client Macintosh**

**Client PC**

**Client PC**

**Token-Ring wiring hub**

**Hub-to-hub link
(fiber optic cable)**

**IBM data connector**

**Shielded or unshielded twisted pair LAN cabling**

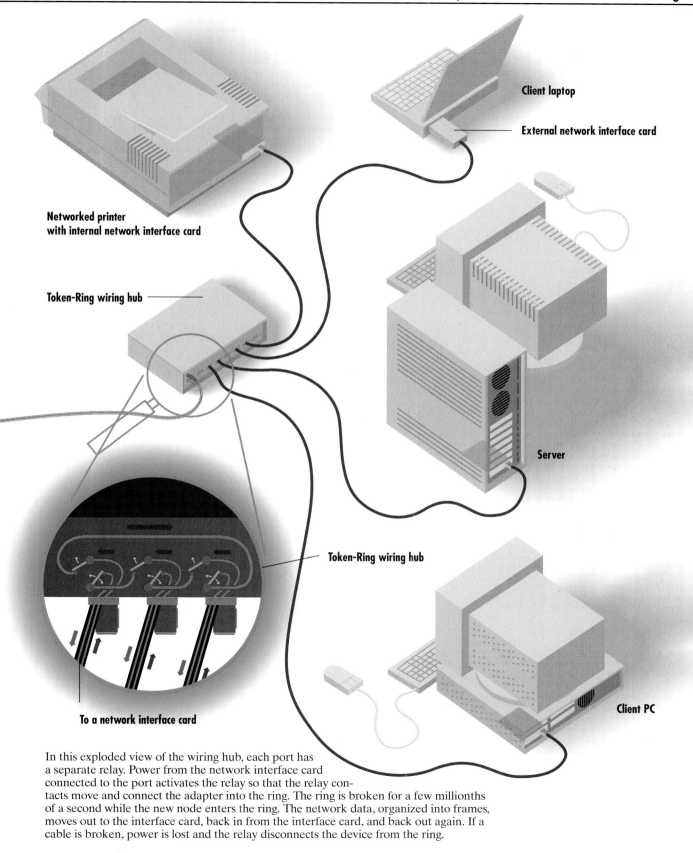

Client laptop

External network interface card

Networked printer
with internal network interface card

Token-Ring wiring hub

Server

Token-Ring wiring hub

To a network interface card

Client PC

In this exploded view of the wiring hub, each port has
a separate relay. Power from the network interface card
connected to the port activates the relay so that the relay con-
tacts move and connect the adapter into the ring. The ring is broken for a few millionths
of a second while the new node enters the ring. The network data, organized into frames,
moves out to the interface card, back in from the interface card, and back out again. If a
cable is broken, power is lost and the relay disconnects the device from the ring.

# ARCnet

ARCnet is a robust and reliable networking system. It uses a star cabling pattern with passive and active hubs that can extend the cabling farther than Ethernet or Token-Ring configurations. Networked devices share the cabling using an orderly polling scheme. The installer sets switches on each network interface card, which gives the card a specific number. The lowest numbered active card becomes a master controller. It sends a message to each adapter in sequence, giving it permission to transmit any data it holds. The standard ARCnet signaling speed of 2.5 Mbps limits the maximum throughput, but the orderly polling scheme raises the average effective throughput. A system called ARCnet Plus, released in 1992, uses 20 Mbps signaling and is compatible with the cabling of the original system.

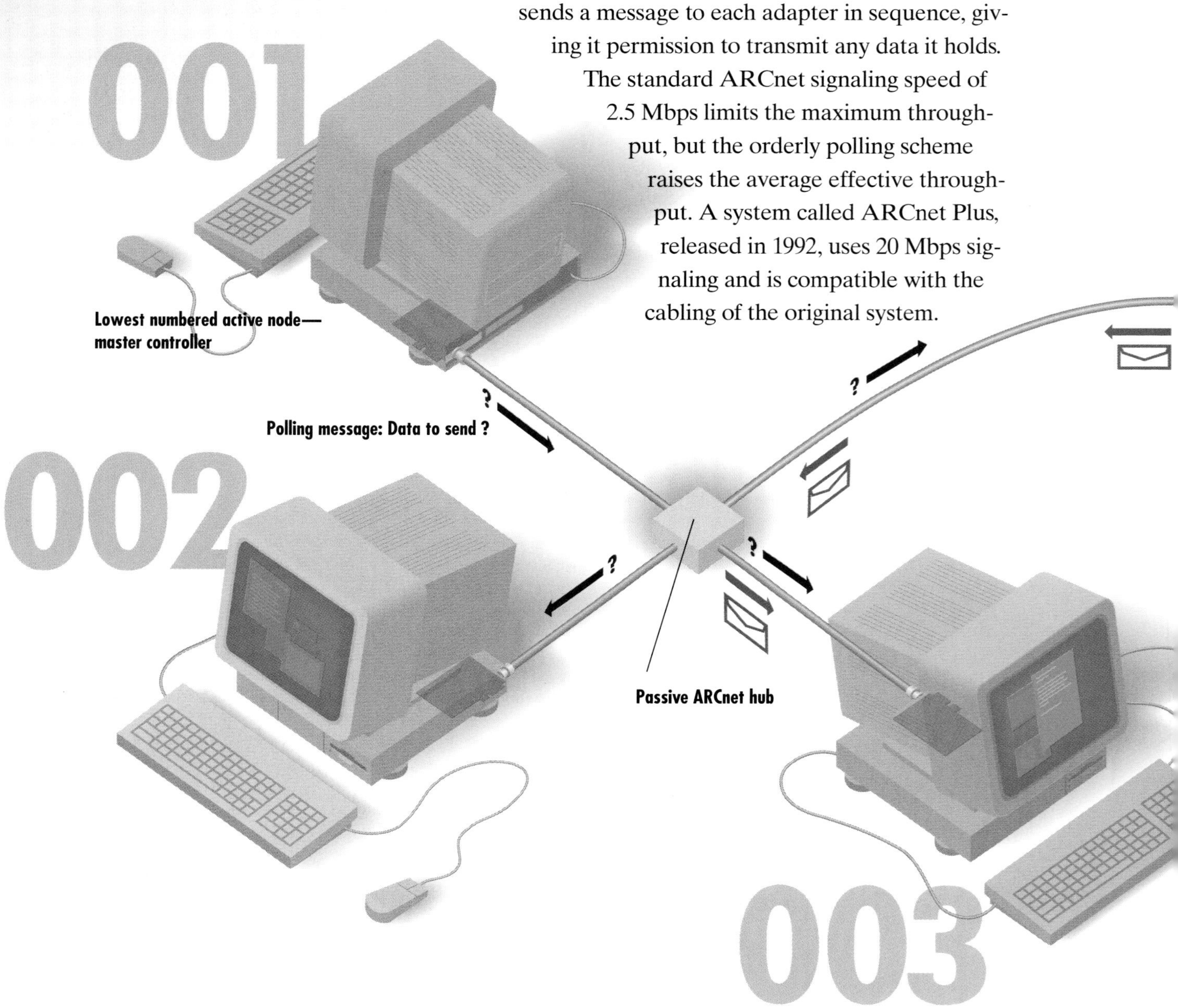

**001**

**Lowest numbered active node—
master controller**

**002**

**Polling message: Data to send ?**

**Passive ARCnet hub**

**003**

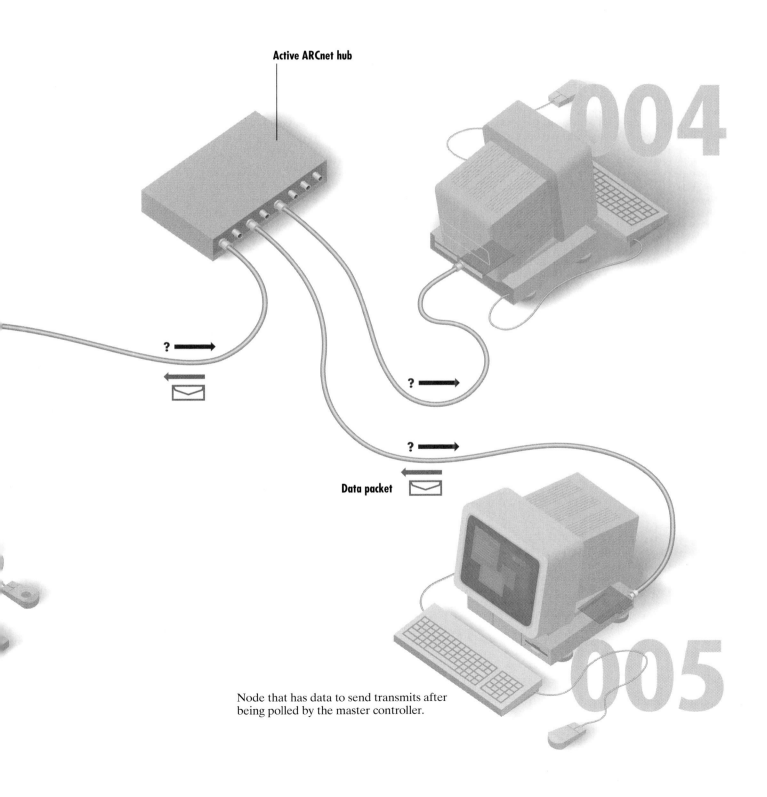

Active ARCnet hub

Data packet

Node that has data to send transmits after being polled by the master controller.

# Structured Wiring System

A structured wiring system provides a standardized way to wire a building for all types of networks. The main distribution frame links all the building's interior wiring and provides an interface connection to circuits coming from outside sources such as the local telephone company. Wiring hubs provide the connection logic unique to Ethernet, Token-Ring, or ARCnet adapters.

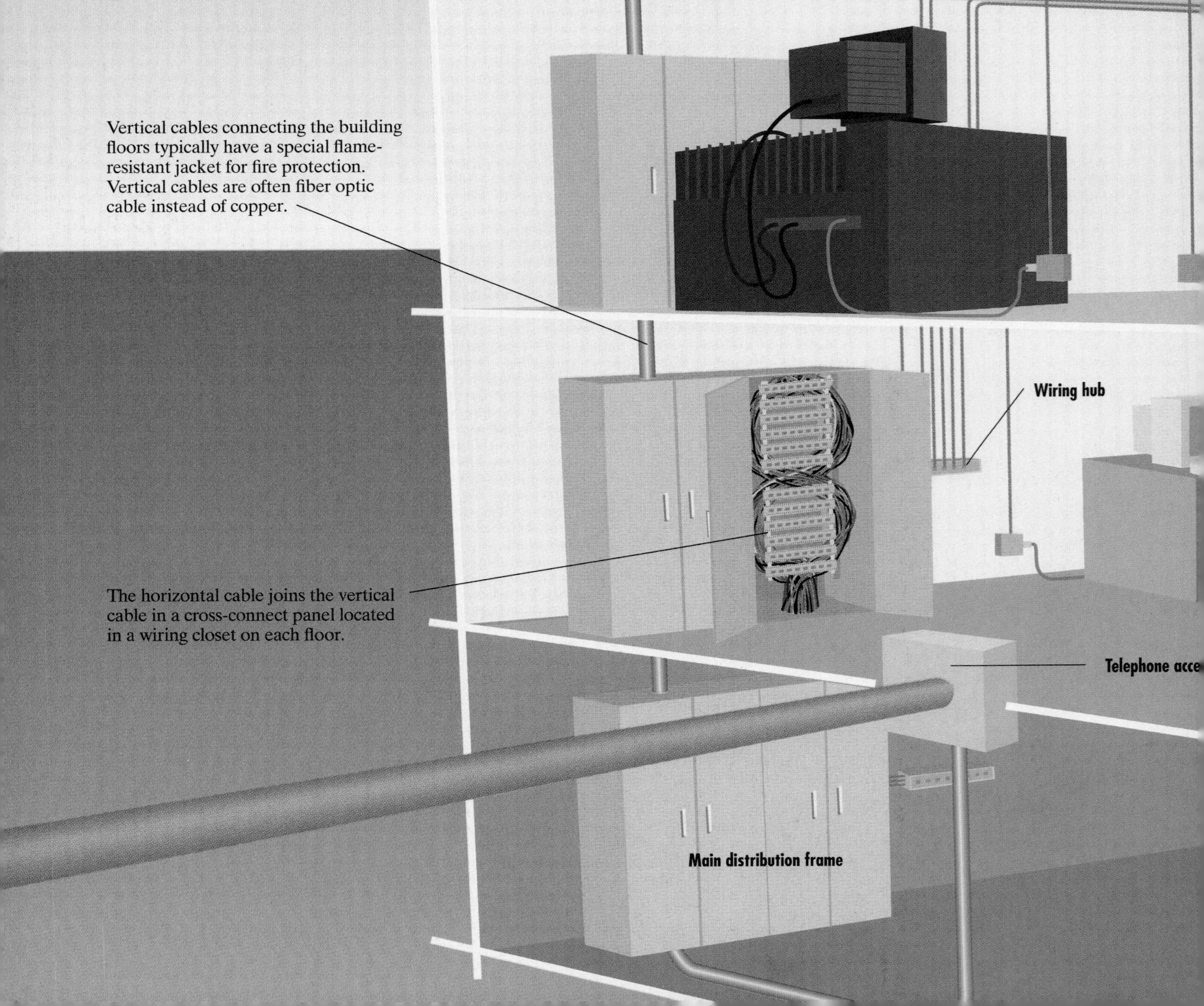

Vertical cables connecting the building floors typically have a special flame-resistant jacket for fire protection. Vertical cables are often fiber optic cable instead of copper.

Wiring hub

The horizontal cable joins the vertical cable in a cross-connect panel located in a wiring closet on each floor.

Telephone acce

Main distribution frame

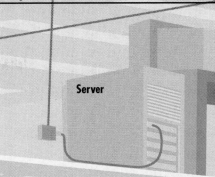

Server

Each floor's horizontal cable—usually unshielded twisted pair copper wire—distributes the network connections to wall jacks near each piece of networked equipment.

Networked printer

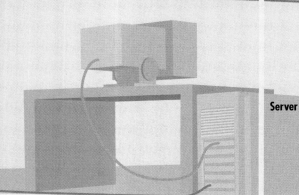

Server

Wall plate

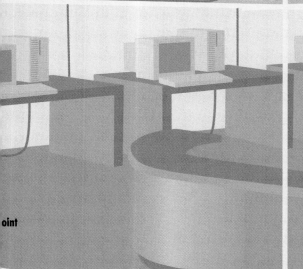

oint

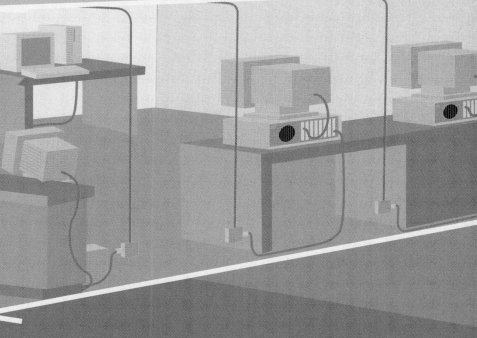

# Wireless Networking

Some networked systems don't use any cables. Wireless network devices extend networks beyond the reach of copper or fiber optic cables. We categorize wireless network devices into those that work within a room or building, those that work across a city, and those that work around the world. Each type of product uses different technology and has different costs and operating speeds, but they all offer portable or mobile computing capability for people on the go.

Local wireless systems extend a wired network to laptop and palm-top computers within a room or building. Small wall-mounted transceivers connect to the wired LAN and establish radio contact with portable networked devices within their broadcast range.

11:00 - Status Report Meeting: OMRI (more)

1:30 - Late lunch with new Ad Agency (more)

3:00 - Call Printing Company, Inc. > Mr. Davis

4:00 - Call daycare > Mrs. Elwain

FAX Melinda re: final changes 17.6 (more)

Download iNET:email-MTDwork (auto)

er with Laurie N (more)

e recieved from N. Voskuil

available for review

sed & ready for review

Michael's PDA STATUS

Cellular Link: OPEN

Fax/Modem: IDLE

Battery: 67%

Processor: 100%

Compression: ON

Sound: ON

6.11.94  2:47pm

appointments

Wireless adapters using cellular telephone technology connect portable and mobile computers scattered across a wide area into their local networks. Small antennas on the back of or within personal computers communicate with radio towers in the surrounding area.

Wireless networking around the world uses satellites in near-earth orbit that can pick up low-powered signals from portable and mobile networked devices.

CHAPTER
18

# Server-Based LANs

THERE ARE THREE types of servers—file servers, print servers, and communications servers—but under different network strategies various devices on the network can also perform these server functions. One network strategy relies on a single powerful computer that is dedicated to providing all server functions for dozens or even hundreds of client computers on the network. This is known as server-based networking.

Another network strategy, known as peer-to-peer networking, distributes the server functions among many computers. They act as file or print servers even while they run application programs such as spreadsheets and databases. We'll describe the pros and cons of peer-to-peer networking in the next chapter.

Server-based networks have a higher start-up cost than peer-to-peer networks and, typically, require more technical expertise to install and manage because of the powerful hardware and software they use. But this strategy benefits from economy of scale; as you install more client computers that share the server's resources, a server-based network becomes more economical.

A computer designed to act as a dedicated file server has cabinet space for more disk drives, a bigger power supply to handle the load, the ability to expand to tens of megabytes of RAM, a fast interface bus, and the fastest affordable processor. It isn't unusual to find a dedicated server equipped with several network interface cards. Each card addresses a separate segment of cabling so that the data-carrying capacity of a single cable doesn't block the use of the server's power.

Server-based systems provide good control, backup, and management of critical data because important records and files reside in one place. The file server runs a multitasking operating system that can execute several programs at the same time, so, while it is saving or opening a file, the server can also record the date and time of the action, check for computer viruses, and flag the file for back up to a tape drive. Management reports from the server software can help network administrators spot the need for more resources, such as disk-drive storage. Server software can even bill individuals and departments for use of the server's resources.

Powerful server-based networks offer security, excellent data management, fast response, and room for expansion. But they are complex and represent a considerable investment in equipment, software, and training.

# Server-Based LAN

A large and powerful computer is the heart of a server-based network. The networked client computers use the file, print, and communications services of the central server. This architecture is robust, powerful, complex, and has a significant installation cost, but as you add more users, the cost-per-user drops.

Client computers

Each client computer runs its own application programs, and networking software in each client computer redirects requests for file and print services to the file server. Files created by the applications, and perhaps the application programs themselves, cross the network from the file server. This network uses several parallel network cable runs to ensure that the client computers can benefit from the fast data handling of the server.

This computer, designed to act as a
central server, is equipped with multiple
hard-disk drives, a tape drive for backup, and a
CD-ROM drive. It uses a specialized multitasking
operating system and runs a variety of management
and monitoring programs, in addition to the file and
print services.

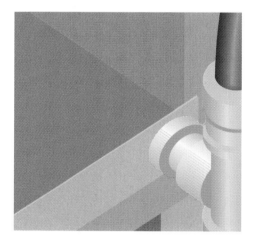

# Peer-to-Peer Networks

I N THE LAST chapter, we described server-based networks that dedicate a computer to act as a file server, print server, and possibly as a communications server, too. In this chapter we'll describe the advantages and disadvantages of peer-to-peer networks, which don't rely on one dedicated server. This strategy shares the processing power and storage capacity of networked computers even while they run application programs.

Peer-to-peer networking makes sense because personal computers seem to defy the laws of supply and demand—their power goes up while their prices go down or at least stay the same. Modern desktop computers have power to spare and to share, so if they are not used heavily to run applications, they become even more valuable as file and print servers. Peer-to-peer networking offers excellent economy because it takes advantage of computer hardware that's already paid for.

In a peer-to-peer network, some computers run file-server networking software in addition to client networking software, application programs, and an underlying operating system. This type of peer-to-peer networking software is a part of the Macintosh operating environment and Microsoft's Windows for Workgroups. However, just because server software is present, a computer's resources are not automatically open to everyone on the network. The person using a particular computer decides what files, subdirectories, or drives are shared across the network. Peer-to-peer network operating systems make it easy to share devices—such as CD-ROM drives, tape drives, and removable cartridge drives—with any other networked computer.

Peer-to-peer network operating systems typically don't have the powerful management and auditing features found in server-based software because that processing power is used by local applications. However, they are easy to install and maintain and provide good responsiveness— particularly if the file read and write load is shared among several computers acting as file servers. It's also possible to combine peer-to-peer networking with a server-based architecture.

Peer-to-peer networks offer a low start-up cost, simplicity, and enough power to satisfy the needs of many organizations.

# Peer-to-Peer Networks

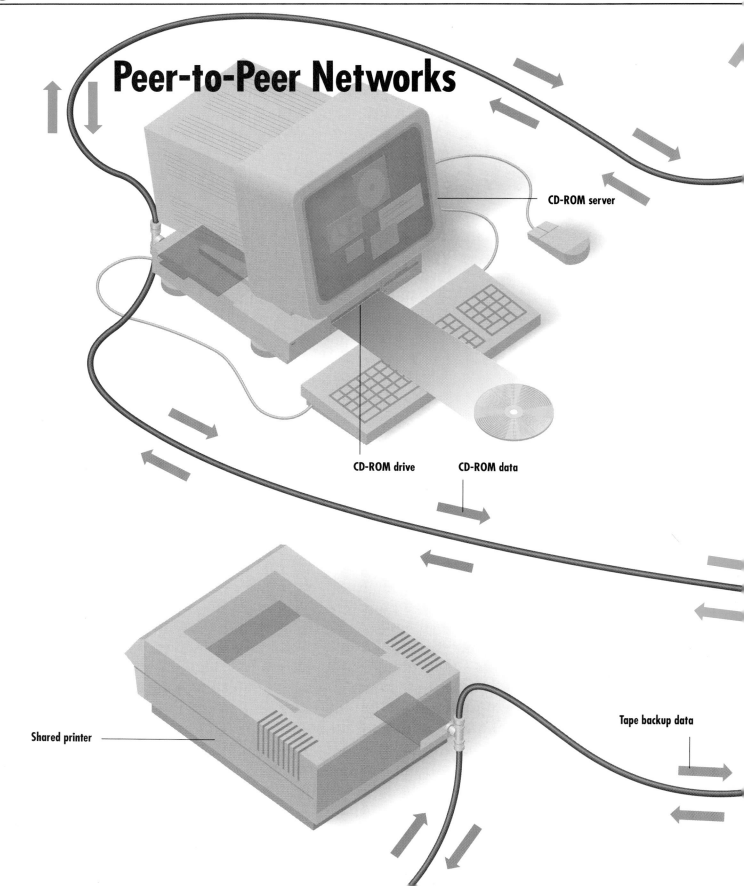

CD-ROM server

CD-ROM drive

CD-ROM data

Shared printer

Tape backup data

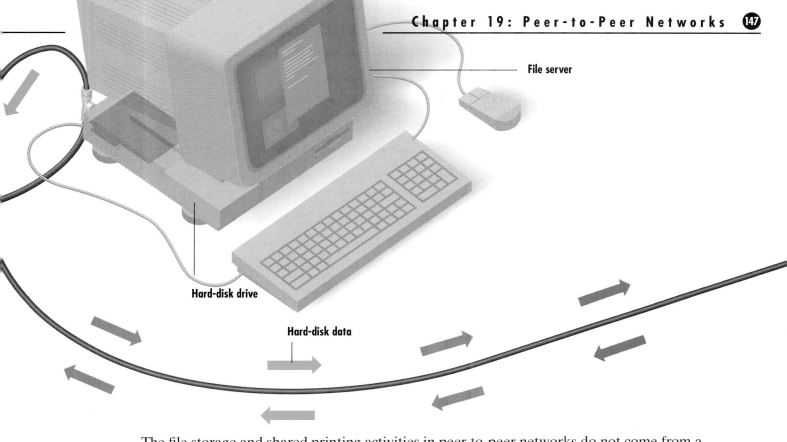

File server

Hard-disk drive

Hard-disk data

The file storage and shared printing activities in peer-to-peer networks do not come from a single server. Instead, any computer on the network can share its drives and printers across the network while running application programs. In this illustration, different computers share their hard-disk drives, tape drive, and CD-ROM drive. This type of network doesn't have the sophisticated management and options found in a server-based system, but it is easy to install and economical. And, it is possible to expand peer-to-peer systems to include a dedicated server as an organization's needs grow.

Tape backup server

Tape drive

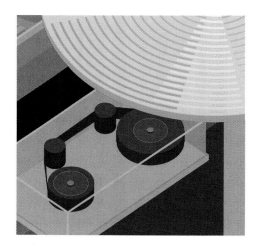

# Network Management

COMPUTER NETWORKS HAVE become the assembly line, warehouse, and delivery system for many organizations, so networks deserve all the management resources once lavished on the forges and furnaces of heavy industry. Network management programs take the place of inspectors with hard hats and flashlights. These programs run in servers, in wiring hubs, and even on network interface cards. They gather statistics on the movement of data and watch for conditions that exceed programmed limits. If they detect a problem, they alert a central management program that can direct certain types of restart or rerouting actions and call for human assistance.

Manufacturers of network equipment have adopted several sets of standards for the operation of network management software. A popular set of standards, the Simple Network Management Protocols (SNMP), serves as a good example for all the systems. Under the SNMP architecture, small management programs, known as *agents*, run in special processors contained in a variety of networked devices. These programs monitor the devices and gather statistical data in a format known as a *management information base* (MIB, rhymes with *bib*). A central program, known as the *management console program*, polls the agents on a regular basis and downloads the contents of their MIBs.

A wiring hub is a very effective location for a management agent. The hub sits at the center of the wiring system and the agent can monitor the level of activity and the type of data moving to and from each client and server. Servers often have their own agents that report more details on the condition of the server and on the actions of the client computers. Management agents are also available for certain models of network interface cards and for specialized products, such as uninterruptable power supplies with network attachments.

Management console programs use graphical maps and representations of the network. Their screens present marching bar graphs showing network traffic at the monitored points. These programs can also send detailed statistical data to database programs for analysis.

If the data coming in from the agents exceeds certain criteria, management console programs can even dial a telephone number and summon human help through a pager. The screen of the management console shows trouble spots with bold flashing colors. Network managers can use the management console to command changes in the network—typically at the wiring hubs.

A network management system adds to the cost of a network and isn't necessary in every organization. A network management system may start out with a little monitoring and reporting, typically from a wiring hub, and then more sophisticated capabilities can be added as needed. If a network is a vital part of an organization, then a network management system is inexpensive insurance for the success of the operation.

# Network Management System

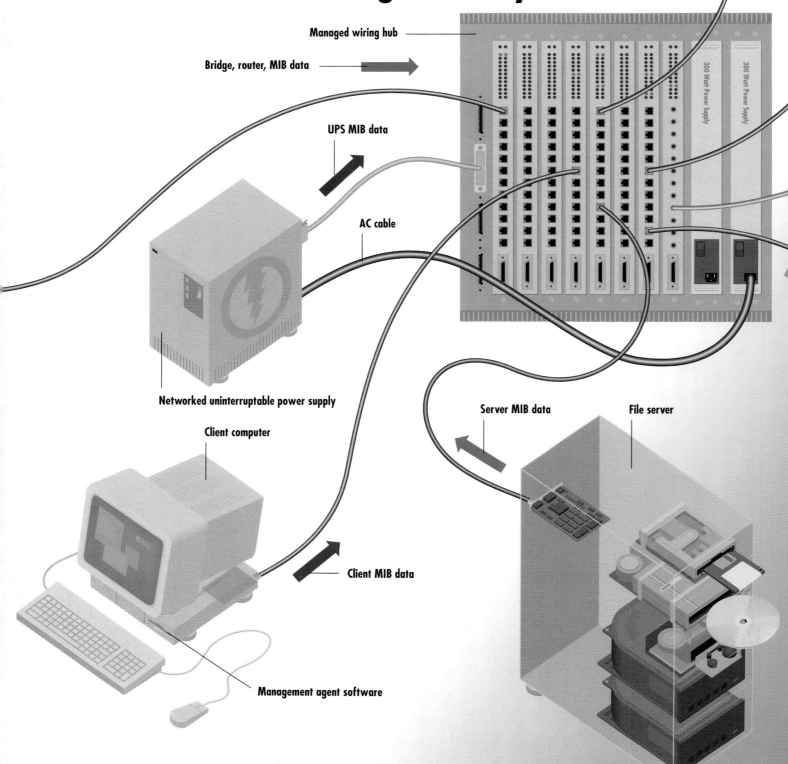

Managed wiring hub

Bridge, router, MIB data

UPS MIB data

300 Watt Power Supply

300 Watt Power Supply

AC cable

Networked uninterruptable power supply

Client computer

Server MIB data

File server

Client MIB data

Management agent software

A network management system uses programs called agents, which run in special processors installed in a variety of networked devices. These programs gather data in a format known as a management information base (MIB) and transfer it to a management console program running in a computer with a highly graphical display. The management console program creates network maps, bar charts, and other informative displays. The console software can automatically order some actions, for example, disconnecting a disruptive computer from the network and notifying a human operator of emergency conditions.

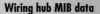 Wiring hub MIB data

Management console screen

# LINKS
# BETWEEN LANS

CONTENTS

NFORMATION IS THE raw material, inventory, and processed product of many modern organizations. Computer networks are the production line, distribution system, and even the retail point of sale for the information products generated by many organizations and businesses. These networks act as local, regional, and international distribution systems for modern commerce.

If local area networks (LANs) are like the in-house production lines of manufacturing plants, then computer networks that cover the distances between cities and countries are the roads and rail lines of modern businesses. Long-distance data networks, called metropolitan area networks (MANs), and wide area networks (WANs) are the equivalent of the trucking, rail, barge, and air freight systems needed to support smokestack industries.

Because many organizations need to move a lot of data over distances greater than a few thousand feet, the industry developed several techniques for extending and linking LANs. The techniques you select to link LAN segments depend on the distance and speed needed, the network communications protocols in use, and your business's philosophy regarding leasing versus owning facilities.

As copper cables extend over long distances, they accumulate electrical noise from the outside environment and from each other. As the pulses of electricity or light representing the data bits travel through copper or fiber optic cables, they lose their sharpness and degrade in strength. Induced noise and signal degradation are the two primary factors that limit, even under the best conditions, the effective length of the high-speed LAN cable to several miles. Long-distance LAN-to-LAN connections move data more slowly than do local connections and require more technical equipment and quality checks.

Just as some manufacturing companies own their own trucks and boxcars, and others contract for all transportation services, some organizations own their MAN and WAN facilities, and others lease these specialized services from commercial suppliers. Many organizations set up their own microwave, light beam, or fiber optic transmission systems to carry data around a metropolitan area or campus. Organizations can use the transportation tunnels under many cities to install their own fiber optic cable systems between their offices or stores and to major customers and suppliers. Metropolitan telephone and cable television companies also supply LAN-to-LAN connections under several types of business arrangements. But when the connections extend beyond the metropolitan area, organizations typically lease circuits from suppliers such as the long-haul telephone carriers AT&T and MCI, specialized companies such as Tymnet and Telenet, and satellite system providers such as GTE.

When you lease circuits for links between LANs, you have many options. The three general technical categories of leased services are *circuit-switched, full-period,* and *packet-switched*. Circuit-switched services are those with a dial tone; for example, switched-56 digital services and the Integrated Services Digital Network (ISDN). The equipment dials a connection, transfers data, and hangs up when it completes the transaction. Full-period services, such as leased telephone lines, provide a circuit dedicated to your use full time. Packet-switched systems—CompuServe, Tymnet, and SprintNet are examples—allow multipoint connections for bursts of short packets. Packet-switched networks are also called X.25 networks after an older CCITT packet-switching standard; today, these networks commonly use a newer standard called frame relay.

To lease a circuit to link LAN segments will cost, typically, thousands of dollars a month. The cost is determined by the maximum signaling speed desired and sometimes by the distance. Therefore, it makes sense to invest in network portal devices for both ends of the link that can use the expensive circuit to maximum efficiency.

Network traffic typically follows specific paths and travels within a group of people with common business interests—a workgroup. However, some traffic also flows between workgroups. Putting all workgroups on the same cable and letting them communicate without restrictions consumes the available resources of the cable. Organizations with busy networks can use network portal devices called bridges that link workgroup LANs while exercising discrimination over the traffic passing between them. Unlike a repeater, which passes all data between cable segments, a bridge links cable systems but passes only certain specified traffic between those systems.

A router is a more complex portal device than a bridge and has a greater ability to examine and direct the traffic it carries. Routers are somewhat more expensive to buy and require more attention than bridges, but their greater efficiency makes them the best choice for a portal between a LAN and a long-distance link. Although the names, basic concepts, and uses of bridges and routers are relatively simple, the selection of one of these products involves enough options to keep a committee busy for a long time.

Bridges can link local cable segments, or the fast cable of a LAN to slower links such as networks of leased telephone lines. The two purposes of a bridge are to extend the network and to isolate network traffic. Like repeaters, bridges can send packets and frames between various types of media. Unlike repeaters, however, bridges forward only that traffic that is addressed to devices on another cable system. This limits the nonessential traffic on all linked cable systems. A bridge reads the destination address of the network packet and determines if it is on the same segment of network cable as the originating station. If the destination station is on the other side of the bridge, the bridge sequences the packet into the traffic on that cable segment.

Local bridges link fast cable segments on a local network. Remote bridges link fast local cables to slower long-distance cables in order to connect physically separated networks. The important point is that you need only one local bridge to link two physically close cable segments, but you need two remote bridges to link two cable segments over a long connecting span of slower media.

Just as bridges are more useful than repeaters, so devices called routers improve on bridges. Routers read the more complex network addressing information in the packet or token and may add more information to get the packet through the network. For example, a router might wrap an Ethernet packet in an "envelope" of data containing routing and transmission information for transmission through an X.25 packet-switched network. When the envelope of data comes out the other end of the X.25 network, the receiving router strips off the X.25 data, readdresses the Ethernet packet, and sequences it on its attached LAN segment.

Routers make very smart connections between the elements of complex networks. Routers can choose from redundant paths between LAN segments and they can link LAN segments using very different data packaging and media access schemes. Primarily because of their complexity, however, routers move data more slowly than bridges.

The links between LANs are easy to understand if you break them into their simplest parts and study a few options. In the next four chapters, we'll describe and diagram the portals and circuits used to link LANs.

PART FOUR

CHAPTER
21

# Repeaters, Bridges, and Routers

**J**UST AS MANUFACTURING plants have mail rooms and shipping docks, local area networks have specified places—called *portals*—where the local and long-distance services meet. Portal devices—repeaters, bridges, and routers—extend and segment the local area network's high-speed cable, and each device offers a different degree of discrimination and data handling capability.

A repeater, typically a little box you can hold in your hand, connects two segments of your network cable; the repeater retimes and regenerates the digital signals on the cable and sends them on their way again. Repeaters are relatively inexpensive and easy to install, but even a string of repeaters can't extend the high-speed LAN cable beyond a few thousand yards.

Bridges and routers are more complex and expensive devices that can be found within personal computers, as stand-alone devices on the LAN, and as modules that are part of wiring hubs. Bridges read the station address of each Ethernet packet or of a Token-Ring frame—the outermost envelope around the data—to determine the destination of the message, but they do not look inside the packet or frame to read NetBIOS, IPX, or TCP/IP addresses.

A router digs deeper into the envelopes surrounding the data to find the destination for the data packet. A router reads the information contained in each packet or frame, uses complex network addressing procedures to determine the appropriate network destination, discards the outer packet or frame, and then repackages and retransmits the data. When routers connect LANs, it doesn't matter what kinds of hardware the LAN segments use and, because multiprotocol routers are available, the LAN segments don't even have to use the same network communications protocols. Because they don't pass, or even handle, every packet or frame, routers act as a safety barrier between network segments. Data packets with errors simply don't make it through the router.

Routers strip off the outer layers of data before they send a packet from one LAN to the other, so they reduce the total number of bits going across the interLAN communications link. The remote router at the receiving end repackages the data into a packet or frame appropriate for its LAN segment. This allows routers to send the information across the interLAN circuit more efficiently than bridges do, and you can use less costly long-distance circuits.

If the two networks use the same network signaling and access-control protocol, such as Ethernet, the networks can be linked with a bridge on each LAN. But if the networks are different—for example, if one uses Ethernet and the other uses Token-Ring—routers would be the best choice because they remove packets formatted for IPX or IP from the lower-level frame and send them across the interLAN link. Routers once were much more complex and expensive than bridges, but the differences between the capabilities of the products have narrowed so that, today, routers are preferred because they put less data on the expensive communications circuit.

# Repeaters, Bridges, and Routers

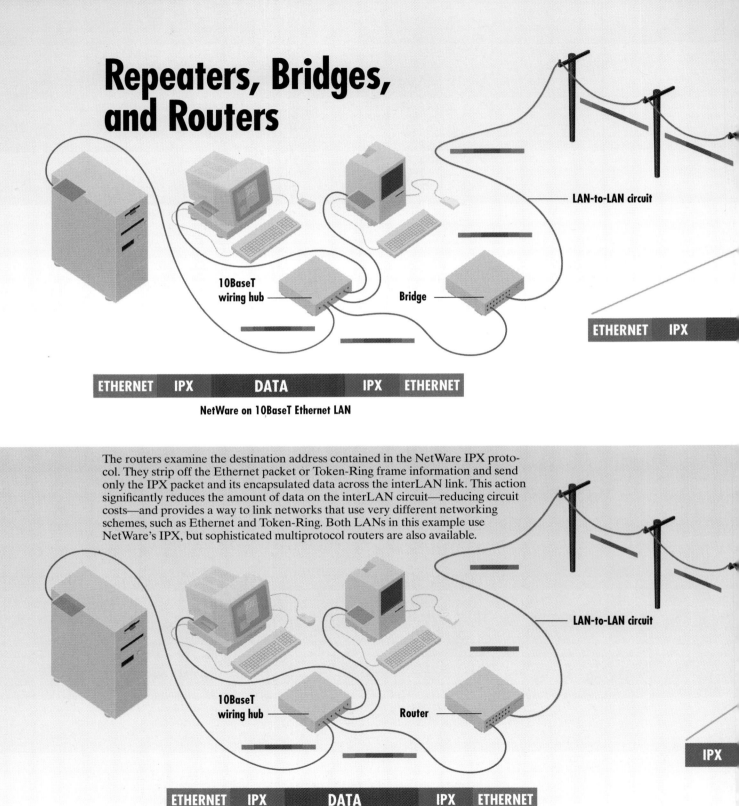

LAN-to-LAN circuit

10BaseT wiring hub

Bridge

| ETHERNET | IPX | | | |
|---|---|---|---|---|

| ETHERNET | IPX | DATA | IPX | ETHERNET |
|---|---|---|---|---|

NetWare on 10BaseT Ethernet LAN

The routers examine the destination address contained in the NetWare IPX protocol. They strip off the Ethernet packet or Token-Ring frame information and send only the IPX packet and its encapsulated data across the interLAN link. This action significantly reduces the amount of data on the interLAN circuit—reducing circuit costs—and provides a way to link networks that use very different networking schemes, such as Ethernet and Token-Ring. Both LANs in this example use NetWare's IPX, but sophisticated multiprotocol routers are also available.

LAN-to-LAN circuit

10BaseT wiring hub

Router

| IPX |
|---|

| ETHERNET | IPX | DATA | IPX | ETHERNET |
|---|---|---|---|---|

NetWare on 10BaseT Ethernet LAN

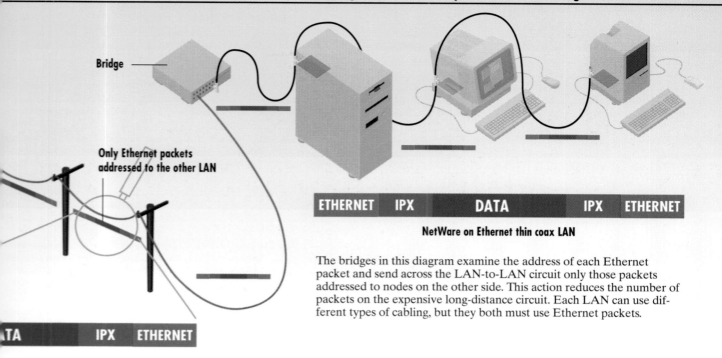

Bridge

Only Ethernet packets
addressed to the other LAN

| ETHERNET | IPX | DATA | IPX | ETHERNET |

NetWare on Ethernet thin coax LAN

| ...TA | IPX | ETHERNET |

The bridges in this diagram examine the address of each Ethernet packet and send across the LAN-to-LAN circuit only those packets addressed to nodes on the other side. This action reduces the number of packets on the expensive long-distance circuit. Each LAN can use different types of cabling, but they both must use Ethernet packets.

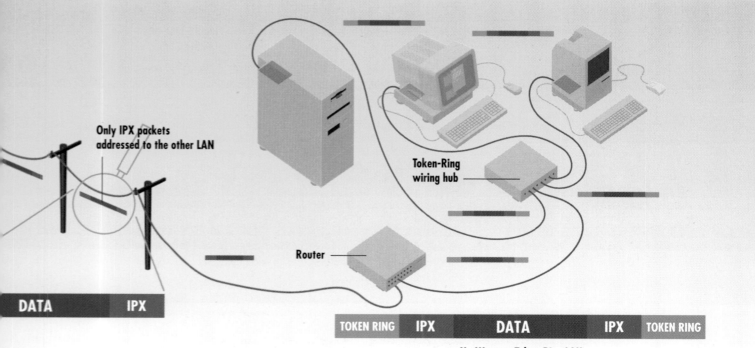

Only IPX packets
addressed to the other LAN

Token-Ring
wiring hub

Router

| DATA | IPX |

| TOKEN RING | IPX | DATA | IPX | TOKEN RING |

NetWare on Token-Ring LAN

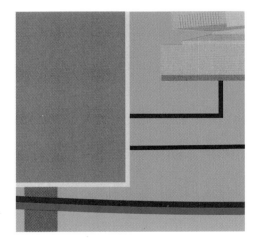

# Metropolitan Area Networks (MANs)

**A**NYONE RUNNING A local area network that supports a business eventually faces the challenge of expansion because LANs are, by definition, local, while businesses try to spread and grow. As businesses and other organizations grow, administrators must find a way to link the LANs within a campus or a city. A metropolitan area network (MAN) presents a unique set of problems and opportunities.

The most common link between networks today is a digital telephone line leased from the local telephone company. But this type of service usually carries signaling speed and mileage charges, and is one of the most expensive links you can buy. There are other, more specialized services designed for data connections.

The IEEE 802.6 committee studies metropolitan area networks. This committee is developing a standard called the Distributed Queue Dual Bus (DQDB). The DQDB topology includes two parallel runs of cable (typically fiber optic) linking each node (typically a router for a LAN segment) on the system. This dual cable system provides high reliability and signaling rates in the range of 100 megabits per second.

The IEEE 802.6 MAN is designed as a metropolitan utility serving a large number of organizations across an area of many miles. In the United States, IEEE 802.6 MANs probably will be installed and run by the local telephone companies.

Another service, called Fiber Distributed Data Interface (FDDI), provides a backbone of communications services across town and can act as a traffic-gathering system to feed the DQDB backbone. FDDI systems have a sustained throughput of about 80 megabits per second and are limited to about 60 miles of cable. Companies can economically install FDDI systems for their own use and to sell as a service to anyone in the extended neighborhood. Many companies sell FDDI network adapters, so they can be used as a local network connection alternative within a building and then extended to the metropolitan environment.

The FDDI architecture uses two rings of fiber to carry data. All nodes attach to the primary ring, but since the secondary ring is designed to provide a backup connection, some nodes (called Class B stations) might not attach to the secondary ring for reasons of economy.

Finally, you can make wireless interLAN connections within a metropolitan area, particularly if you have at least one office with a top-down view of the skyline. Several companies—including M/A-Com, MicroWave Networks, Inc., and Motorola Microwave— sell microwave radios operating at 23 gigahertz (GHz) that can be, literally, pointed out the window toward the distant LAN. Microwave is a reasonably economical option for distances of up to 20 miles: it offers signaling speeds of 1.544 megabits per second and, at a typical cost of $10,000 to $15,000 per set, there are no monthly leased-line charges.

You would usually lease metropolitan area LAN-to-LAN circuits from your telephone company and from other vendors. But installing your own links is an excellent alternative for many organizations.

# Metropolitan Area Networks

The organization in this well-connected office building extends its local area network using digital
circuits leased from the local telephone company,
microwave radio connections to a nearby operating
location, and an FDDI network to three LANs in the
metropolitan area.

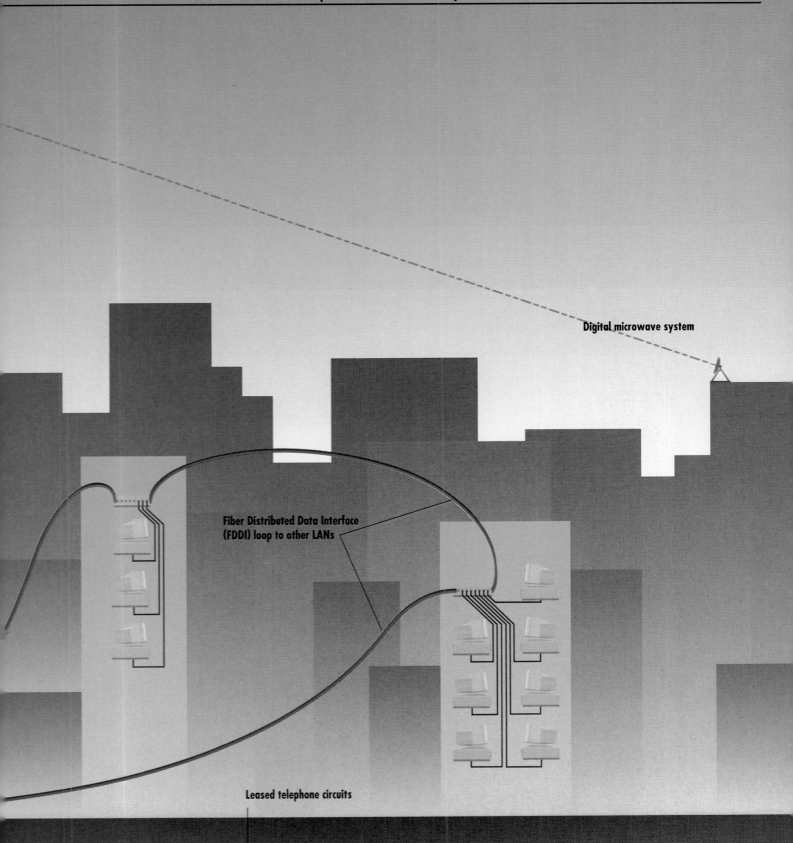

Digital microwave system

Fiber Distributed Data Interface
(FDDI) loop to other LANs

Leased telephone circuits

# Circuit-Switched Digital Services

**T**HE LAWS OF physics dictate that a signal degrades as it passes over a cable. Network engineers have to employ expensive equipment and techniques to preserve data integrity and move that data quickly over long distances. The formula is *speed × distance = cost.* You can trade off signaling speed and distance to hold down costs, but if you must have high signaling speed over a long distance, it will be expensive.

Instead of paying for LAN-to-LAN links on a full-time basis, you can dial up digital connections as you need them. Circuits that you dial up to make a connection are called circuit-switched digital services. Generally, a circuit-switched digital service is more economical than a leased line service if you need connections for only three to eight hours a day, or less. Circuit-switched digital services are perfect for linking electronic-mail servers on different LANs and for doing tasks such as updating inventory and order records from one network database to another at the end of each day.

The major portions of the public telephone systems are fully digital. They handle voice and data as a stream of 0s and 1s instead of analog tones. Only the last few miles of cable carry data in analog form. The only difference between the circuit-switched voice connection of phone calls and the circuit-switched data connections occurs in the cable between the telephone company's central office and the termination. Voice circuits use an older type of wiring system meant to eliminate distortion of the voice. Modems for voice circuits convert data to tones that traverse a few miles of cable until they become data again at the central office. When telephone companies install switched digital services, new wiring systems carry the data in digital form all the way and there is no need for modems.

Circuit-switched service vendors offer dial-up circuits able to carry maximum signaling rates of 56, 64, and 384 kilobits per second and 1.544 megabits per second. Switched data circuits follow the same pricing scheme as switched voice circuits. You pay for equipment and installation, a monthly service charge, and for each call by the minute according to the distance. In some areas, switched-56 service costs no more than voice service.

The Integrated Services Digital Network (ISDN) is a circuit-switched digital service. ISDN marketing literature stresses combined voice and data applications, but companies such as Digiboard and Microcom market practical ISDN routers for LAN-to-LAN services. These devices establish an ISDN circuit-switched digital connection between appropriate LANs when traffic appears, and then break down the connection when it is no longer needed.

The most popular ISDN service for linking LANs is basic rate interface, or BRI. This service delivers two data channels able to carry 64 kilobits per second each, called bearer channels, or B channels, and a separate 16-kilobit-per-second channel, called the data channel, or D channel. The D channel is used to signal the computers in the telephone switching system to generate calls, reset calls, and receive information about incoming calls, including the identity of the caller.

Circuit-switched digital services can provide handy and economical connections between LANs. They are a useful alternative to metropolitan and long-distance inter-LAN connections.

# Circuit-Switched Digital Network

**Central office switches**

The central office of every local telephone company is a computerized switch that works with other similar switches to route and complete a call—that's where the term *circuit switching* comes from.

A switching matrix connects local access lines and long-distance services on a temporary per-call basis.

**Digital local access circuits**

**LAN ROUTER**

Digital access equipment connected to a router calls the central office switch. ISDN equipment uses a separate 16-megabit channel for fast call setup. Other switched services use standard dialing tones.

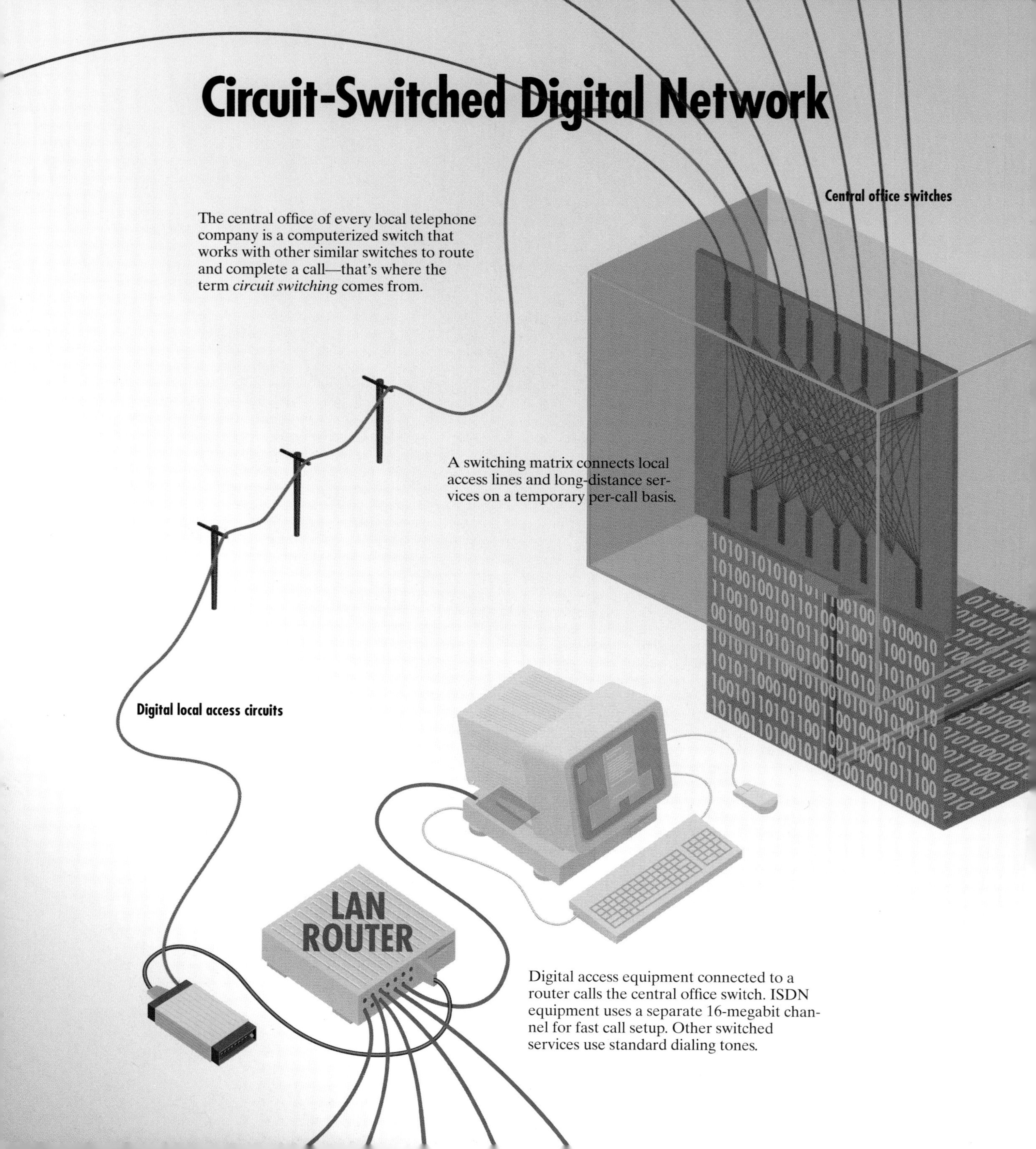

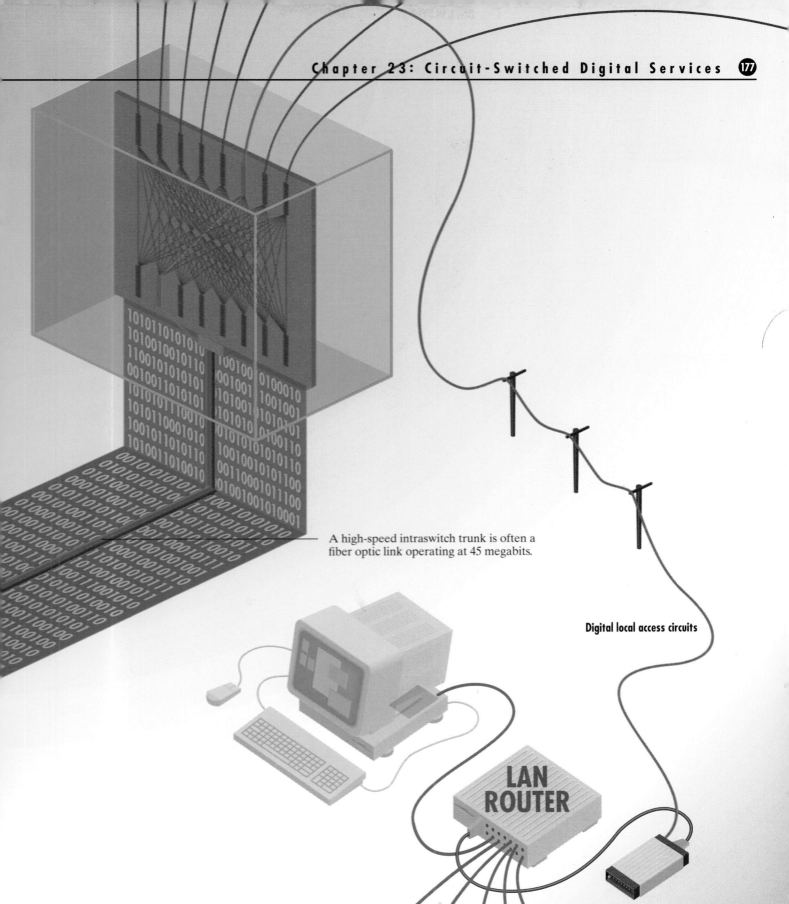

A high-speed intraswitch trunk is often a
fiber optic link operating at 45 megabits.

Digital local access circuits

LAN
ROUTER

# Packet-Switching Networks

**A**NOTHER TECHNOLOGICAL ALTERNATIVE for LAN-to-LAN connections are packet-switching networks. This category includes X.25, frame-relay, and cell-relay technologies. Packet switching is more popular in Europe and Asia than in the United States because many U.S. organizations depend on leased-line services.

The major appeal of packet-switching services comes from their flexible multipoint capabilities. LANs in many different locations can exchange data with one central location and with each other. The LAN portals can use different signaling rates and the packet-switched network buffers the data. Commercial packet-switching networks are also called public-data networks (PDNs)—or value-added networks (VANs)—because of the error-control, buffering, and protocol conversion they can provide. The most common examples of packet-switching networks are CompuServe and MCI Mail.

Although the other LAN-to-LAN alternatives typically involve flat monthly fees, packet-switching networks are, in a term of the trade, *usage sensitive*. That is, you pay a basic monthly service charge and a fee based on the amount of data received by each of your ports on the network. Usage-sensitive billing can make packet-switching networks more attractive than full-period leased lines when your applications transfer data only a few times a day.

Full-period connections to the packet-switched network are available from your network portal device, and usually operate at rates of 56 kilobits through 1.544 megabits per second. The carrier you choose can make all the arrangements for the service and present the charges in one bill.

Until 1991, a protocol called X.25 dominated packet-switched networks. This protocol uses a belt-and-suspenders design to ensure the delivery and integrity of data shipped across the network. But networks using reliable digital circuits don't need all the accounting and checking provided by the X.25 protocols, so designers stripped off many X.25 functions, reduced the overhead, and developed a service called frame relay. Several standards organizations adopted important frame-relay standards in 1991 and some vendors first offered frame-relay service intermixed with X.25. Today, newcomers such as MCI Data Communications don't even offer X.25 service—the focus is now on frame relay.

New developments in packet-switched systems center on cell-switching technologies. Because the X.25 packet and the frame-relay frame are of variable length, the network must constantly adjust the flow and timing of messages. If the data bundles are all the same size, the network designers can tighten up the operation, gaining efficiency and reducing the complexity of the system. A technology generally called cell relay and an evolving cell-relay standard called asynchronous transfer mode (ATM) are designed for very heavy data loads. Operating at speeds of 1.544 megabits per second to 1.2 gigabits per second, ATM cells consist of 48 bytes of application information plus 5 bytes for the header. Network equipment can quickly route and move these uniformly sized bundles of data.

Packet-switched systems offer reliability and flexibility for LAN-to-LAN connections. There is little up-front cost, and you can have service where you need it, when you need it, and for only as long as you need it.

# Packet-Switching Network

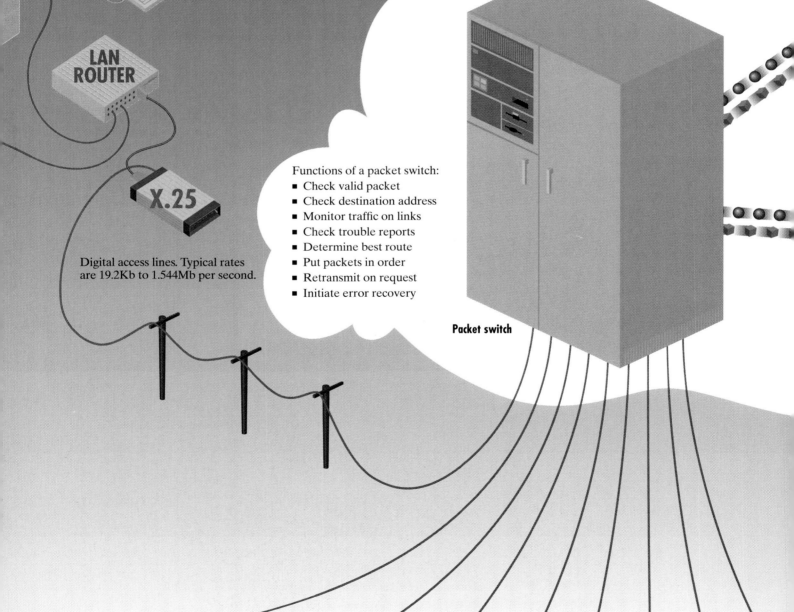

**LAN ROUTER**

**X.25**

Digital access lines. Typical rates are 19.2Kb to 1.544Mb per second.

Functions of a packet switch:
- Check valid packet
- Check destination address
- Monitor traffic on links
- Check trouble reports
- Determine best route
- Put packets in order
- Retransmit on request
- Initiate error recovery

**Packet switch**

**Packet switch**

Intraswitch trunks provide alternative
paths to ensure network reliability.

Each packet contains addressing, routing,
timing, checksum, and other network
information. Frame-relay packets contain
less recovery information. If a frame-relay
packet is lost or damaged, higher-level
programs retransmit the data.

**Packet switch**

**Digital access lines**

**X.25**

**LAN ROUTER**

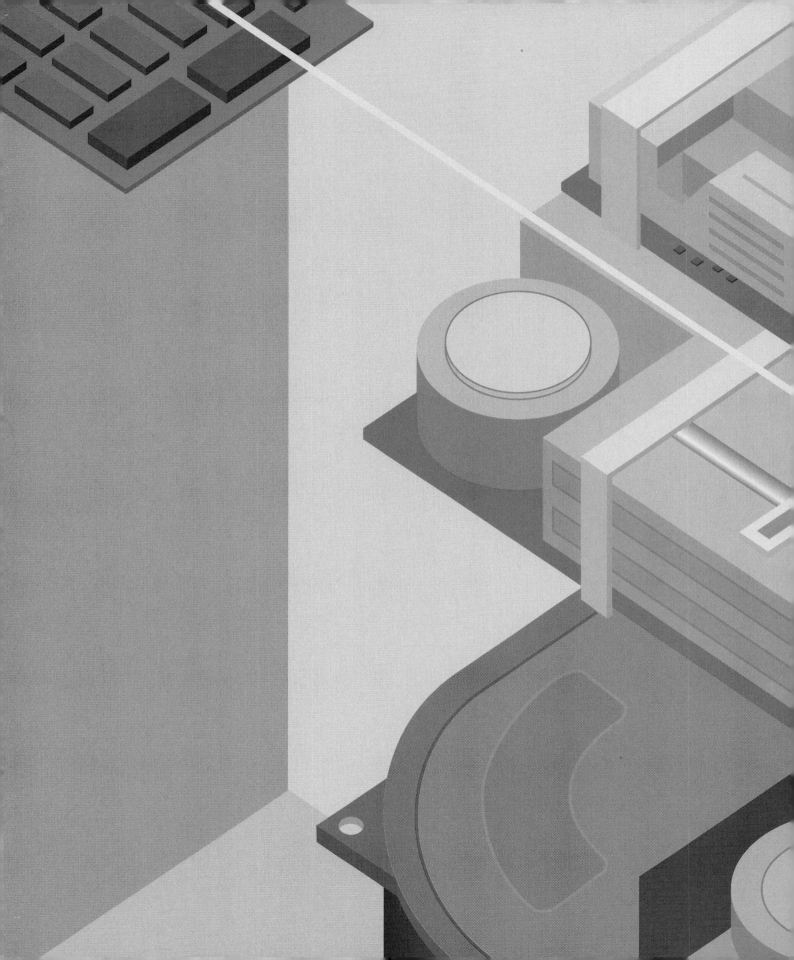

# WORKGROUP APPLICATIONS

## CONTENTS

A NETWORK IS particularly useful for *workgroups*—people working together on common projects. A network makes it easy for people to collaborate on a project for a short time, perhaps just hours or days, and then move on to another task with a different workgroup, without even changing desks. This flexibility to form virtual workgroups is important in keeping costs down in modern organizations.

Workgroup networking changes the way people work and allows organizations to change their own structures. As more people interact across the network, the organization needs less administrative overhead. Coordination takes place at the personal level with less bureaucratic involvement. The network budget grows as the administrative support budget gets smaller—and the result is more productivity. One advantage of this change is that organizations can choose if they want to own or lease the added networking capabilities.

Workgroup networking has three major components: connectivity, messaging, and client/server actions. *Connectivity* refers to the links between the network elements—particularly the LAN adapters and cabling.

*Messaging* is the ability of the network to accept, store, and deliver messages from one user or application program to another. Messages are often simple typed notes—electronic mail—exchanged between coworkers, but messages can also be sophisticated automated interactions that occur between programs as they update and share information. Some applications use network messaging services to update and exchange shared information—such as workgroup scheduling, where a central calendar is kept for coordinating the actions of people and equipment, and project tracking, for managing responsibilities and actions.

Several types of servers were described earlier in this book, but the term *client/server* has a slightly different context here. *Client/server action* refers to a task—for example, indexing and finding data in large files—that the file server and client computer share. For example, document management, a type of workgroup application, combines messaging with client/server actions to hold, index, and retrieve specific phrases from the documents used by law offices, insurance companies, and other organizations.

Connectivity and messaging are two functions that companies can install for themselves or lease—many organizations do both. Service companies such as MCI, CompuServe, and AT&T allow corporate and private subscribers to connect to their packet-switched networks instead of installing expensive private links between local area networks. These subscription connections provide reliability, flexibility, and pay-as-you-go pricing. Organizations can mix and match connections—subscription, owned, and leased—to meet their long- and short-term connectivity needs.

MCI, CompuServe, AT&T, and other companies also offer messaging services to subscribers. These services accept messages and files, store them, convert them to different formats, copy them into different accounts, and deliver them on demand. The basic service is often called electronic mail, but the underlying messaging service is the foundation for much more sophisticated interactions. MCI, CompuServe, AT&T, and other companies offer access to information services such as databases of business news and statistics, searchable archives of articles, and specialized electronic libraries. These companies also provide a way for businesses to reach out electronically to their dealers and customers with current information and even to deliver updated versions of software products.

Electronic-mail systems can be set up on local area and wide area networks. A few companies include electronic mail as a part of their network operating system packages. Typically, though, e-mail software, the equipment to run it, and someone to take care of it must all be paid for, so subscriber-based electronic-mail systems have some advantages.

You can set up another type of store-and-forward system for electronic messaging called a bulletin board system (BBS). This is a single computer, often with a tie to a local area network, that accepts outside calls, holds messages and files, and delivers them to the appropriate subscribers. The BBS you install and manage can have many of the same information database, library, and distribution functions that are available from subscription services.

Client/server computing is important because it allows PC and Macintosh computers to access very large libraries of data without drowning in the information or swamping the network. In the client/server network architecture, the client computer sends a generalized request for information to the file server. Special software in the file server interprets the generalized request, takes the detailed steps (such as extensive indexing and sorting) needed to fill the request, and delivers the final results to the client computer. Using client/server techniques, applications running on client computers with modest processing power that are connected by slow long-distance circuits can have detailed and efficient access to huge information databases. Client/server techniques are important to workgroup productivity programs because many such programs operate in a monitoring, or background, mode. They share the computer's processing power with other programs such as spreadsheets and word processing products. Client/server techniques allow the workgroup productivity programs to regularly access a lot of information without taking computing power away from other active applications.

Workgroup productivity applications such as electronic mail, scheduling, project management, and document management rely on the network for connectivity and such services as messaging and database access. In turn, people in organizations rely on these applications to make their work more efficient and effective. Networks and workgroup productivity software are important tools for modern commerce.

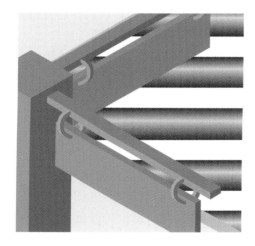

# On-line Information Services

**A**S THE PERSONAL computer evolved from a hobbyist's toy to a mainstream business machine, it left a trail of new industries. One of the most intriguing of those new industries is the on-line information service.

On-line information services such as CompuServe, Prodigy, and America Online are sources of information available via a modem. Subscribers to these services pay, typically, a monthly fee for basic access, plus additional charges for more specialized services. Several major information companies provide a broad array of services to the computing public: a wealth of information on stocks and bonds, news, sports, and computing. In a sense, on-line information services act as a giant electronic funnel. They gather news and information from other sources around the world and offer that information to their subscribers.

Most information services operate on large mainframe computer systems. An extensive network of modems and leased telephone lines allows subscribers to access the host system via a local telephone call.

Prodigy and CompuServe are the most popular services; each has over a million users and is owned by a large corporation. CompuServe is a division of H&R Block, the income-tax giant, and Prodigy is owned by a joint venture of IBM and Sears.

Prodigy began life as Trintex, a joint venture of CBS, Sears, and IBM. Prodigy was based on the then-popular notion that most American homes would have a home computer of some type by the late 1980s. The joint venture would use IBM's technological prowess, CBS's entertainment connections, and Sears's retail know-how.

CBS, citing financial difficulties, dropped out of the project before the service began operations. IBM and Sears pressed on, changing the name to Prodigy, but maintaining the basic idea of a consumer-oriented, inexpensive on-line service. Prodigy offers a broad array of services, many of which are aimed at households with children. Prodigy's monthly flat-fee pricing was a first in an industry accustomed to charging by the minute.

CompuServe began by appealing to the hard-core computer hobbyists in the mid to late 1970s. The demographics of computer users have changed radically over the years, and CompuServe now offers a balanced selection of financial, information, and entertainment services. But CompuServe has managed to keep the more technically oriented users happy, too. CompuServe's Forum software allows a group of users to exchange messages and files related to a common topic. These forums—or electronic bulletin boards—began as an electronic meeting place for computer hobbyists, but they have grown to encompass a wide range of topics. For example, there are CompuServe forums dedicated to IBM-compatible computers, model railroading, aquarium keeping, personal investing, and world events. Because CompuServe's network extends to many locations in Europe and the Far East, you can exchange messages with other members worldwide.

# On-line Information

The CompuServe information service is actually a network of networks. CompuServe collects and stores data from a number of sources, including the Associated Press news and sports wire services, stock-market and commodity exchanges, and dozens of specialized information services.

Users from around the world connect via modem to CompuServe's host computer in Ohio. From their computer screens and keyboards, the users can view or download any of the information stored on CompuServe's system.

The CompuServe forums provide two-way communication among users. Forums operate much like an e-mail system, but all messages on a forum are visible to all forum users. This open-air approach allows for ongoing group discussions. Many computer hardware and software vendors operate CompuServe forums as part of their customer support efforts.

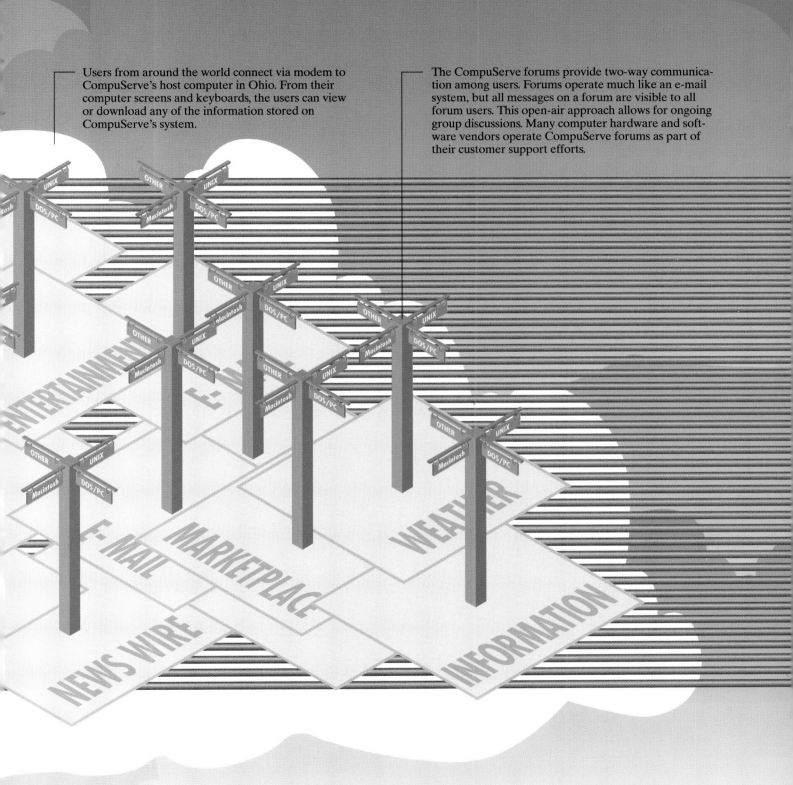

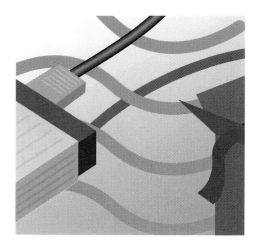

# Electronic-Mail Systems

ELECTRONIC-MAIL SYSTEMS—or e-mail, as they are commonly called—store messages and deliver them when the addressees are ready to receive them. These store-and-forward services partially replace telephone calls and face-to-face meetings and offer their own unique system of workgroup interaction. Electronic-mail programs allow widespread organizations to overcome the limits of time zones and office hours.

Electronic mail can do many jobs: create, read, forward, reply to, track, and log messages. Some of the most useful features in an electronic-mail system include pop-up windows for reading messages, a text editor for message preparation, such options as importing text files into messages and attaching files (for example, spreadsheets) to outgoing messages, and return-receipt service for messages. Also, electronic-mail programs on LANs often have the ability to exchange messages among dissimilar mail systems.

In an electronic-mail system, software in each computer reads and writes to a shared set of subdirectories in the network file server. Each electronic-mail subscriber runs a program that checks the files in the subdirectories for waiting mail. In large networks connected by LAN-to-LAN links, each LAN might have its own set of electronic-mail message files, which is generally called a post office. One computer on each LAN, called the postmaster, on a regular basis runs a program that identifies messages destined for other post offices, collects them, and forwards them.

Either the postmaster or another computer on the network can run a program that identifies messages destined for other electronic-mail systems or services that use a different message format or addressing structure. This computer performs a function—it provides a *gateway*. It translates the message formats and addresses, makes a connection (typically through a modem) to the other mail system or service, and exchanges messages. For example, gateways are typically available for links between LAN electronic-mail systems and services such as MCI or AT&T mail. Gateways also make it possible for people to send fax messages. Because of gateways and separate post-office systems, you can create one message with a variety of internal electronic-mail, external mail service, and fax addressees.

People working outside the office need to have access to the electronic-mail system, so vendors typically offer a special remote-access program. If the electronic-mail company doesn't sell a special piece of software, you can easily use a modem remote-control program to set up a remote-entry communications server. Callers run the LAN electronic-mail program on a remote networked personal computer, read the screen, create replies, and use the file transfer abilities of the remote-control program to transfer any attachments. This technique also keeps all the mail on the network while providing full services.

An electronic-mail program simplifies information-sharing tasks for its users and avoids the problem of telephone tag. Large systems entail many complexities, but links between electronic-mail products allow you to mix and match electronic-mail systems throughout your organization to meet specific needs. An electronic-mail system is the foundation for a strong and practical information-sharing system in your LAN.

# Electronic Mail

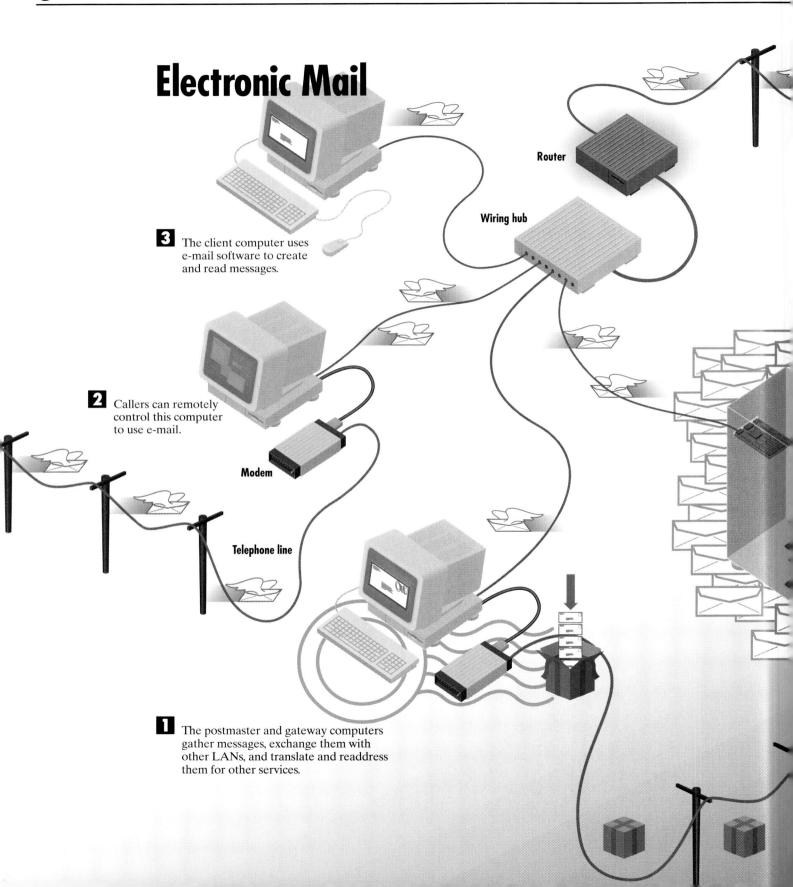

**Router**

**Wiring hub**

**3** The client computer uses e-mail software to create and read messages.

**2** Callers can remotely control this computer to use e-mail.

**Modem**

**Telephone line**

**1** The postmaster and gateway computers gather messages, exchange them with other LANs, and translate and readdress them for other services.

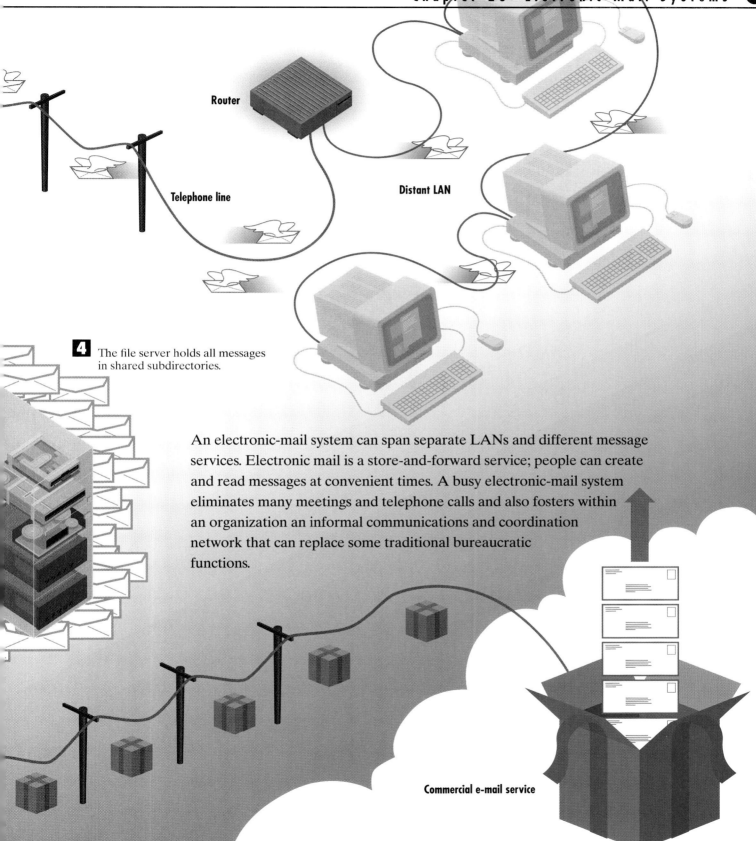

**Router**

**Telephone line**

**Distant LAN**

**4** The file server holds all messages in shared subdirectories.

An electronic-mail system can span separate LANs and different message services. Electronic mail is a store-and-forward service; people can create and read messages at convenient times. A busy electronic-mail system eliminates many meetings and telephone calls and also fosters within an organization an informal communications and coordination network that can replace some traditional bureaucratic functions.

**Commercial e-mail service**

# MCI Mail

MCI Mail can relay messages to and receive messages from virtually any telex or TWX machine worldwide. This allows users to send and receive telex messages, even if they don't have telex machines.

MCI operates several print sites worldwide where your e-mail message can be printed and mailed, usually for next-day delivery. MCI even operates a printed-mail courier service in some major cities, allowing users to send nearly instant e-mail to people who don't even have computers.

The President announced today the successful agreement by all parties to an International Free Trade and Business Act. Seven countries endorsed the plan, including the United

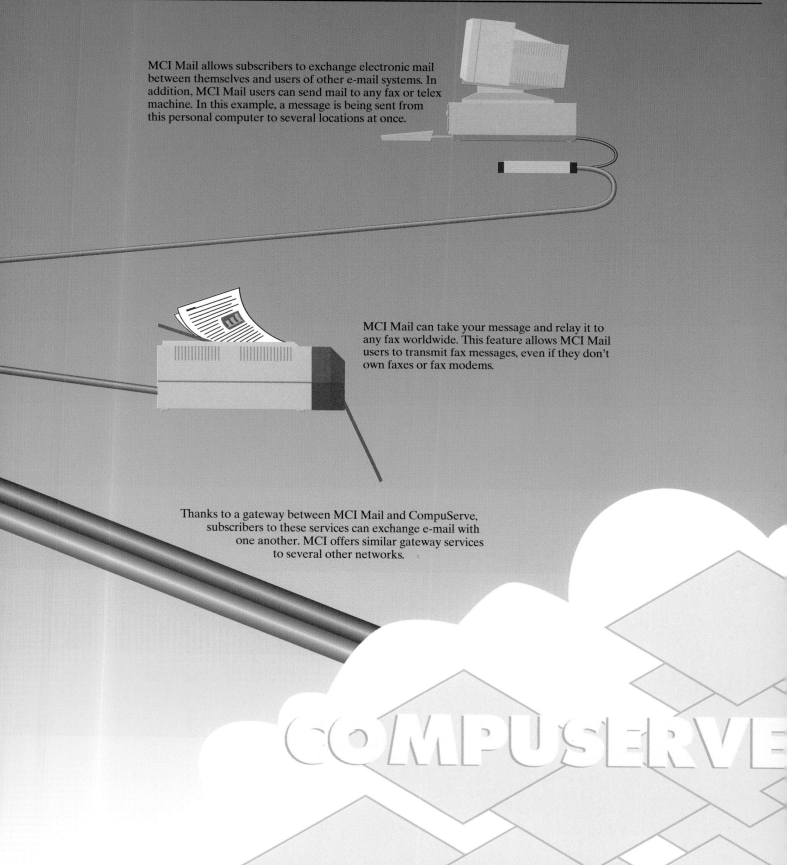

MCI Mail allows subscribers to exchange electronic mail between themselves and users of other e-mail systems. In addition, MCI Mail users can send mail to any fax or telex machine. In this example, a message is being sent from this personal computer to several locations at once.

MCI Mail can take your message and relay it to any fax worldwide. This feature allows MCI Mail users to transmit fax messages, even if they don't own faxes or fax modems.

Thanks to a gateway between MCI Mail and CompuServe, subscribers to these services can exchange e-mail with one another. MCI offers similar gateway services to several other networks.

COMPUSERVE

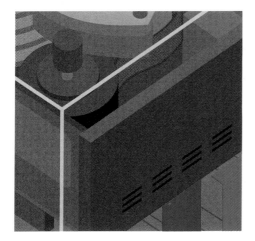

# Client/Server Computing

I N PREVIOUS CHAPTERS we described several types of servers and clients, so what is so different about the client/server computing architecture described in this chapter? The phrase *client/server computing* refers to sharing the work between the client and the server so each device performs the tasks it can do most efficiently. You see the best example of client/server computing in database management systems.

In older database technology, each desktop computer runs a database program that calls for large data files from the file server, spends time sorting and searching the files, and then generates a report with the desired information. The newer client/server model distributes the task. The client computer sends a request to a special program called a *database engine*—running in the file server— which indexes, sorts, and searches the shared files without sending them over the network. The database engine, or database server as it's also known, responds with only the specific files or results requested by the client computer. While the database engine does its work, the client computer can give its resources to running other applications.

The client/server model makes it possible to produce useful yet small programs for desktop computers. Because the programs are small, they can stay resident in desktop computers and provide on-call capabilities. Some of the most interesting client/server applications fall into the category of workgroup applications. Workgroup applications use the database server as a shared pool of information. These workgroup programs help people to store and retrieve documents, to schedule appointments, to manage major projects, and to control and schedule the flow of work within an organization.

The concept of forms processing is fundamental to the new vision of workgroup productivity. The term *forms* is very broad and touches every aspect of the interaction of people in business, government, and academic workgroups. Some forms, like mail routing slips, remain as paper throughout their useful life. But other forms, such as credit application forms, are typically only the first step toward entry into a computer database. Many forms, such as receipts and invoices, are the paper output of computer systems. The simple goal of workgroup software is to automate the forms—all forms—so they never become paper and then to route the forms electronically, often along multiple paths simultaneously, to speed and manage the process. But it takes the processing power of a database engine and the structured approach of the client/server architecture to make this goal practical.

The person using the desktop computer typically uses an on-screen form to specify the request. In a document management system, the form might allow the user to request a search of a library of documents to find a specific group of documents by using the author's name, a few words inside each document, or other criteria as the search key. The software in the desktop computer translates the form into a request using the *Structured Query Language* (SQL), a database language originally developed by IBM and now in wide use. The database engine in the file server runs through all the files using the search key, compiles the results, and then returns either the actual files or the statistical results to the client computer.

Client/server computing, forms processing, and forms routing are the foundation for many workgroup applications, and workgroup productivity applications simplify, automate, and integrate sharing across networks.

# Client/Server Database System

Client/server database systems divide the workload. The database engine software, running in the file server, responds to queries from the client computer software by conducting detailed searches and returning only the results of the searches. Older types of database systems move all the data across the network to each client for processing.

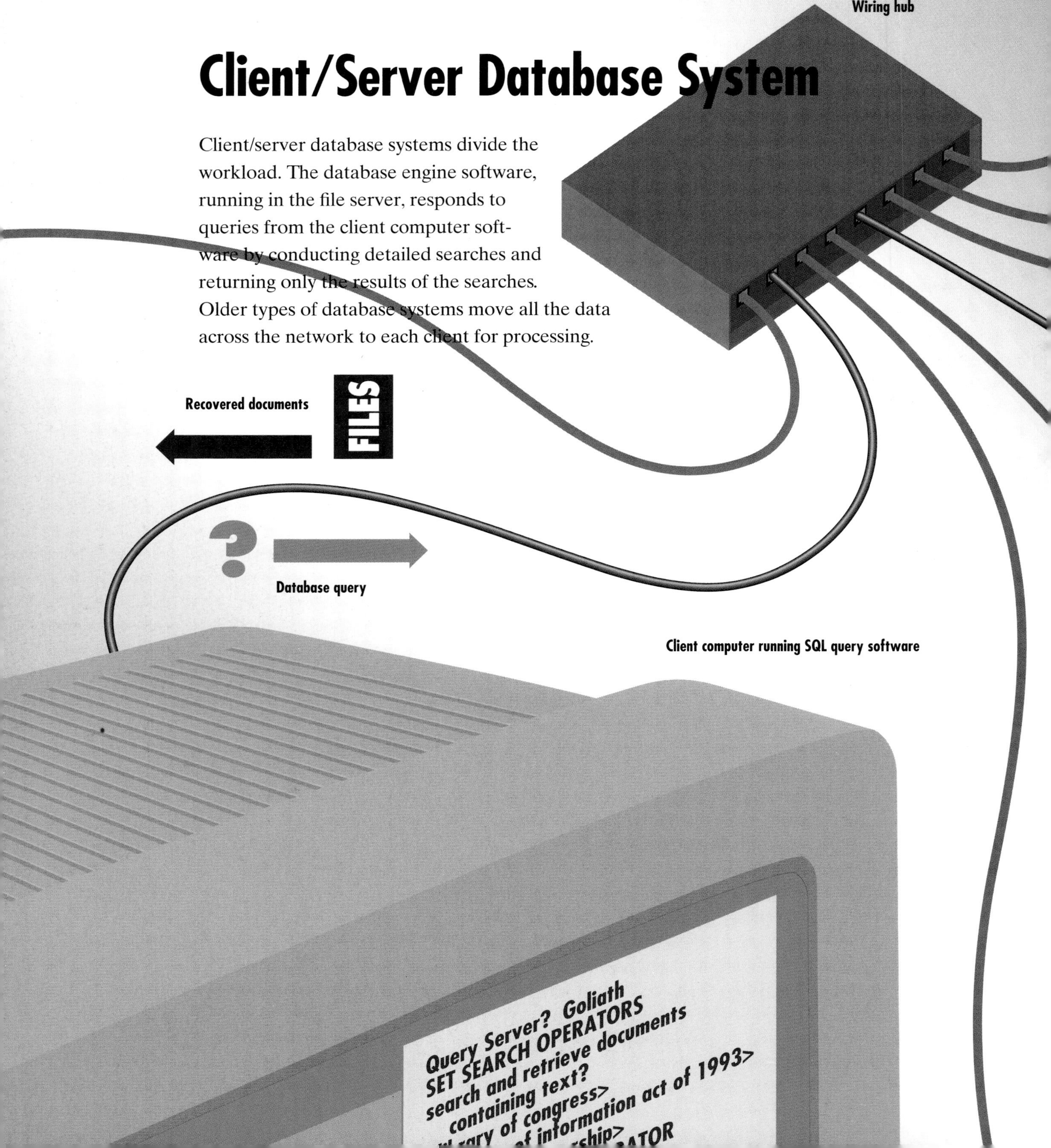

**Wiring hub**

**Recovered documents**

**FILES**

**?**

**Database query**

**Client computer running SQL query software**

Query Server? Goliath
SET SEARCH OPERATORS
search and retrieve documents
containing text?
library of congress>
information act of 1993>
ship> ATOR

PROCESS

INDEX

MERGE

REPORT

PROCESS

SORT

INDEX

Database engine software indexes and
searches files in response to client request

FILES

?

CPU

File server and database engine software

# Imagination.
# Innovation. Insight.

## The How It Works Series from Ziff-Davis Press

*". . . a magnificently seamless integration of text and graphics . . ."*

Larry Blasko, The Associated Press, reviewing *PC/Computing How Computers Work*

No other books bring computer technology to life like the *How It Works* series from Ziff-Davis Press.

Lavish, full-color illustrations and lucid text from some of the world's top computer commentators make *How It Works* books an exciting way to explore the inner workings of PC technology.

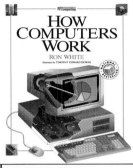

ISBN: 094-7 Price: $22.95

### PC/Computing How Computers Work

A worldwide blockbuster that hit the general trade bestseller lists! *PC/Computing* magazine executive editor Ron White dismantles the PC and reveals what really makes it tick.

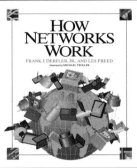

ISBN: 129-3 Price: $24.95

### How Networks Work

Two of the most respected names in connectivity showcase the PC network, illustrating and explaining how each component does its magic and how they all fit together.

ISBN: 166-8 Price: $15.95
Available: October

### How Macs Work

A fun and fascinating voyage to the heart of the Macintosh! Two noted *MacUser* contributors cover the spectrum of Macintosh operations from startup to shutdown.

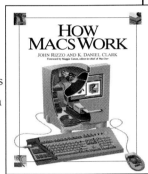

ISBN: 146-3 Price: $24.95

### How Software Works

This dazzlingly illustrated volume from Ron White peeks inside the PC to show in full-color detail how software breathes life into the PC. Covers all major software categories.

ISBN: 133-1 Price: $24.95
Available: October

### How to Use Your Computer

Conquer computerphobia and see how this intricate machine truly makes life easier. Dozens of full-color graphics showcase the components of the PC and explain how to interact with them.

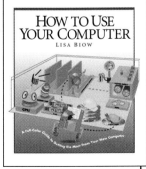

### All About Computers

This one-of-a-kind visual guide for kids features numerous full-color illustrations and photos on every page, combined with dozens of interactive projects that reinforce computer basics, making this an exciting way to learn all about the world of computers.

ISBN: 155-2 Price: $19.95
Available: September

ZIFF-DAVIS
ZD PRESS

**Available at all fine bookstores or by calling 1-800-688-0448, ext. 100.**

# Attention Teachers and Trainers

# NOW YOU CAN TEACH FROM THIS BOOK!

ZD Press now offers instructors and trainers
the materials they need to use this book in their classes.

- An Instructor's Manual features flexible lessons designed for use in a 10- or 15-week course (30-45 course hours).

- Student exercises and tests on floppy disk provide you with an easy way to tailor and/or duplicate tests as you need them.

- A Transparency Package contains all the graphics from the book, each on a single, full-color transparency.

These materials are available only to qualified accounts.
For more information contact:

In the U.S.A:
Academic Institutions: Suzanne Anthony, 800-786-6541, ext. 107
Corporations, Government Agencies: Cindy Johnson, 800-488-8741, ext. 107
In Canada: Copp Clark Pitman Ltd.
In the U.K.: The Computer Bookshops
In Australia: WoodLane Pty. Ltd.

ZIFF-DAVIS
ZD
PRESS

# MAXIMIZE YOUR PRODUCTIVITY WITH THE TECHNIQUES & UTILITIES SERIES

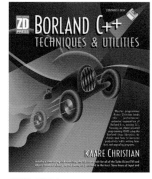

ISBN: 054-8
Price: $39.95

## Borland C++ Techniques & Utilities

Master programmer Kaare Christian leads this performance-oriented exploration of Borland C++, version 3.1. Focusing on object-oriented programming using the Borland class libraries, he shows you how to increase productivity while writing lean, fast, and appealing programs.

## PC Magazine DOS 6 Techniques & Utilities

Based on his national bestseller *PC Magazine DOS 5 Techniques and Utilities*, Jeff Prosise puts essential tools and techniques into your hands with this power-user's guide to DOS 6. The two disks are packed with 60 powerful utilities created specifically for this book.

ISBN: 095-5
Price: $39.95

Techniques & Utilities Series book/disk resources from Ziff-Davis Press are designed for the productivity-conscious programmer or power user. Expert authors reveal insider techniques and have written on-disk utilities and support files so you can apply new skills instantly. If you're a serious programmer or user who wants to get things done quickly and work more effectively, then these are the ideal guides for you.

Look for more performance-oriented titles in the months ahead.

ISBN: 035-1
Price: $39.95

ISBN: 010-6
Price: $39.95

ISBN: 008-4
Price: $29.95

## PC Magazine Turbo Pascal for Windows Techniques & Utilities

Neil J. Rubenking guides programmers through the power and intricacy of programming in Turbo Pascal for Windows. Included are two disks that contain all the source code examples from the text.

## PC Magazine Turbo Pascal 6.0 Techniques & Utilities

This is the ideal guide for serious users who want to get things done. Neil J. Rubenking reveals tips and techniques that will enable you to unleash the full power of Turbo Pascal 6.0.

## PC Magazine BASIC Techniques & Utilities

This guide presents an unprecedented level of coverage of BASIC's internal operation for the QuickBASIC and BASIC 7 programmer. Ethan Winer reveals insider techniques that will allow you to dramatically increase your productivity with BASIC.

ZIFF-DAVIS
ZD
PRESS

**Available at all fine bookstores, or by calling 1-800-688-0448, ext. 102.**

# The Quick and Easy Way to Learn.

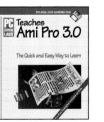

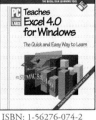

# Ziff-Davis Press Survey of Readers

Please help us in our effort to produce the best books on personal computing.
For your assistance, we would be pleased to send you a FREE catalog
featuring the complete line of Ziff-Davis Press books.

## 1. How did you first learn about this book?

Recommended by a friend . . . . . . . . . . . . . . ☐ -1 (5)

Recommended by store personnel . . . . . . . . ☐ -2

Saw in Ziff-Davis Press catalog . . . . . . . . . . . ☐ -3

Received advertisement in the mail . . . . . . . ☐ -4

Saw the book on bookshelf at store . . . . . . . . ☐ -5

Read book review in: _____ ☐ -6

Saw an advertisement in: _____ ☐ -7

Other (Please specify): _____ ☐ -8

## 2. Which THREE of the following factors most influenced your decision to purchase this book? (Please check up to THREE.)

Front or back cover information on book . . . ☐ -1 (6)

Logo of magazine affiliated with book . . . . . . ☐ -2

Special approach to the content . . . . . . . . . . ☐ -3

Completeness of content . . . . . . . . . . . . . . . ☐ -4

Author's reputation. . . . . . . . . . . . . . . . . . . . ☐ -5

Publisher's reputation . . . . . . . . . . . . . . . . . ☐ -6

Book cover design or layout . . . . . . . . . . . . . ☐ -7

Index or table of contents of book . . . . . . . . ☐ -8

Price of book . . . . . . . . . . . . . . . . . . . . . . . ☐ -9

Special effects, graphics, illustrations . . . . . . ☐ -0

Other (Please specify): _____ ☐ -x

## 3. How many computer books have you purchased in the last six months? _____ (7-10)

## 4. On a scale of 1 to 5, where 5 is excellent, 4 is above average, 3 is average, 2 is below average, and 1 is poor, please rate each of the following aspects of this book below. (Please circle your answer.)

| | | | | | | |
|---|---|---|---|---|---|---|
| Depth/completeness of coverage | 5 | 4 | 3 | 2 | 1 | (11) |
| Organization of material | 5 | 4 | 3 | 2 | 1 | (12) |
| Ease of finding topic | 5 | 4 | 3 | 2 | 1 | (13) |
| Special features/time saving tips | 5 | 4 | 3 | 2 | 1 | (14) |
| Appropriate level of writing | 5 | 4 | 3 | 2 | 1 | (15) |
| Usefulness of table of contents | 5 | 4 | 3 | 2 | 1 | (16) |
| Usefulness of index | 5 | 4 | 3 | 2 | 1 | (17) |
| Usefulness of accompanying disk | 5 | 4 | 3 | 2 | 1 | (18) |
| Usefulness of illustrations/graphics | 5 | 4 | 3 | 2 | 1 | (19) |
| Cover design and attractiveness | 5 | 4 | 3 | 2 | 1 | (20) |
| Overall design and layout of book | 5 | 4 | 3 | 2 | 1 | (21) |
| Overall satisfaction with book | 5 | 4 | 3 | 2 | 1 | (22) |

## 5. Which of the following computer publications do you read regularly; that is, 3 out of 4 issues?

Byte . . . . . . . . . . . . . . . . . . . . . . . . . . . . . . . ☐ -1 (23)

Computer Shopper . . . . . . . . . . . . . . . . . . . . . ☐ -2

Corporate Computing . . . . . . . . . . . . . . . . . . ☐ -3

Dr. Dobb's Journal . . . . . . . . . . . . . . . . . . . . . ☐ -4

LAN Magazine . . . . . . . . . . . . . . . . . . . . . . . ☐ -5

MacWEEK . . . . . . . . . . . . . . . . . . . . . . . . . . ☐ -6

MacUser . . . . . . . . . . . . . . . . . . . . . . . . . . . . ☐ -7

PC Computing . . . . . . . . . . . . . . . . . . . . . . ☐ -8

PC Magazine . . . . . . . . . . . . . . . . . . . . . . . . . ☐ -9

PC WEEK . . . . . . . . . . . . . . . . . . . . . . . . . . . ☐ -0

Windows Sources . . . . . . . . . . . . . . . . . . . . . ☐ -x

Other (Please specify): _____ ☐ -y

**Please turn page.**

6. What is your level of experience with personal computers? With the subject of this book?

|  | With PCs | With subject of book |
|---|---|---|
| Beginner | ☐ -1 (24) | ☐ -1 (25) |
| Intermediate | ☐ -2 | ☐ -2 |
| Advanced | ☐ -3 | ☐ -3 |

7. Which of the following best describes your job title?

Officer (CEO/President/VP/owner) ☐ -1 (26)
Director/head ☐ -2
Manager/supervisor ☐ -3
Administration/staff ☐ -4
Teacher/educator/trainer ☐ -5
Lawyer/doctor/medical professional ☐ -6
Engineer/technician ☐ -7
Consultant ☐ -8
Not employed/student/retired ☐ -9
Other (Please specify): _____ ☐ -0

8. What is your age?

Under 20 ☐ -1 (27)
21-29 ☐ -2
30-39 ☐ -3
40-49 ☐ -4
50-59 ☐ -5
60 or over ☐ -6

9. Are you:

Male ☐ -1 (28)
Female ☐ -2

Thank you for your assistance with this important information! Please write your address below to receive our free catalog.

Name: _____

Address: _____

City/State/Zip: _____

**Fold here to mail.**

1293-07-08

_____

_____

_____

**BUSINESS REPLY MAIL**

FIRST CLASS MAIL     PERMIT NO. 1612     OAKLAND, CA

POSTAGE WILL BE PAID BY ADDRESSEE

**Ziff-Davis Press**
ZIFF-DAVIS ZD PRESS
5903 Christie Avenue
Emeryville, CA 94608-1925
Attn: Marketing

NO POSTAGE
NECESSARY
IF MAILED IN
THE UNITED
STATES

Cut Here

Cut Here